# The Instrument Pilot's Library
## • Volume Two •

# Weather for the IFR Pilot

by
The Editors of *IFR* and *IFR Refresher*

**Belvoir Publications, Inc.**
Greenwich, Connecticut

ISBN: 1-879620-17-0

Printed and bound in the United States of America by Arcata Graphics, Fairfield, Pennsylvania.

# Contents

# Preface

In this second volume of the Instrument Pilot's Library, our goal is to give you greater insight into that favorite topic of instrument pilots, the weather.

Unfortunately, many pilots don't have as much real practical weather knowledge as they should. Part of it comes from the way in which we're trained: when you're paying an instrument instructor all that money, you want to be in the airplane practicing skills, not jawboning about cold fronts. As a result, most pilots wind up getting their weather knowledge from textbooks and hard-won experience.

In this book, our editors and contributors pass on their knowledge, based on many years and thousands of hours in the air, dealing with bad weather.

In the first section, we talk about briefings: How to get more information out of the briefings you're getting now, how to supplement that information with alternative weather sources, and go over in detail how best to use weather charts.

Section two discusses survival in bad weather. We cover the most important skill of all, judgment; followed by a discussion of avoidance tools and strategies to keep you clear of (and help you survive and encounter with) thunderstorms and icing.

Lastly, Section three takes a close look at what makes the weather we fly through, and covers in detail individual weather phenomena, from microbursts to rime icing.

*Weather for the IFR Pilot* is not a weather textbook. Rather, think of it as a tactical manual, a practical handbook for staying ahead of, and out of the way of, severe weather.

# • Section One •

# Preparing Yourself

# Briefing
# Strategies

What's the best way for a pilot to gather weather information? There really isn't one single "best" method, but any good briefing strategy will have a few vital components included in it.

In this first chapter we'll take a general look at the briefing process and go over some of the methods a pilot can use to gather weather information. Later, we'll cover in detail some of the specific reports and charts produced by the National Weather Service (NWS) and the National Oceanographic and Atmospheric Administration (NOAA), or weather "products." And, in a later section of the book, we'll look at specific briefing strategies to get a handle on seasonal weather hazards, like summer thunderstorms and winter icing conditions.

## The time factor

The basis of any safe IFR flight is knowledge about the weather along your route. Arming yourself with as much of it as possible is the only way to make intelligent decisions about your course of action.

Many pilots base their decisions on a single call to Flight Service, or a single session with the FAA computerized briefing service, DUATS. This can serve well in many situations, but a pilot is missing the opportunity to make a more informed choice by not gathering a more complete picture of the weather.

A fundamental characteristic of weather is that it changes over time, often very rapidly. It's important to get not only the "snapshot" of current conditions and forecasts offered by a briefing, but to try and get a broader picture that includes what the weather has been doing over time.

There are, of course, many ways to accomplish this. The following is one good one that makes use of alternate information sources as well as Flight Service. It's the strategy used by a 15,000-hour ATP we know. (There are reasons certain pilots stick around long enough to accumulate that much experience, and being cautious about the weather is one of them.)

## Briefing plan

If you have a flight planned, get acquainted with the air mass picture one or two days before by watching *A.M. Weather* and the cable weather channels. That way you can see the maps and check on frontal movement. Studying newspaper weather maps and forecasts can also be helpful. Also check with flight service for an outlook for your departure and ask for a review of the significant weather prog charts, which indicate weather expectations 48 hours in advance.

Four to six hours before departure, call flight service and get a complete briefing. Discuss possible alternatives at this time. This gives you time to make other arrangements if any severe weather might interfere. It also allows you to check the accuracy of the forecast as the time to planned departure gets closer. Also discuss with the briefer what some of the other NWS products indicate.

If all the data leads you to believe that there won't be any severe weather along your planned route, file a flight plan. If need be, discuss other routes with the briefer before filing. This includes avoidance of thunderstorms and icing. If thunderstorms are in the forecast, ask the briefer to check stations along your route to find out if any have popped up.

One hour before departure, make one more call to see if there has been any change since the earlier briefing. Ask again where thunderstorms (if forecast) have been reported along the route. Ask the briefer to check real-time radar and tell you where cells are located. You can then change your route or destination or alternate accordingly.

After departure, listen to Flight Watch to pick up information from other aircraft. After an hour or so, call the nearest FSS to give a pirep and ask for the latest hourly observations and any updated or amended forecasts. Unless the weather is well above marginal conditions, it's a good idea to ask for this data every other hour thereafter. You can also check with Flight Watch for any data that you did not obtain from FSS.

## Plenty of information

A pilot who uses this overall strategy has a lot of information to work with. Four separate contacts have been made with flight service, along with cross-checks of other information sources ranging from the local newspaper to televised weather. That pilot is unlikely to encounter any nasty surprises en route.

## Briefing sources

There are several ways a pilot can get an official briefing. Four have emerged as the most common: The face-to-face meeting with a FSS specialist (increasingly rare), use of a computer and modem to access DUAT, weather by fax, and the most common, the telephone briefing.

The four briefing sources really fall into two classes: "live," in which the pilot actually talks to someone who can help him or her make sense of the weather situation, and "on-line," where it's entirely up to the pilot to decide which information to retrieve and how to make the best use of it.

A prudent pilot will make use of as many of these information sources as possible. For example, a call can be made to DUAT to gather the raw data, a few fax charts can be ordered, and the whole thing capped off by a phone call to the nearest AFSS.

## "Live" briefings

Once upon a time there were many flight service stations, and it was easy to walk in and talk to a real, live human being about the weather, take a look at the charts, and file your flight plan. With the shrinking number of stations, it's more difficult to do that, but still worthwhile if you have the chance.

Now, of course, the most common means of obtaining a weather briefing is via telephone. Much of the methodology is the same as for a visit to the flight service station, so we won't treat them separately here. The biggest difference is that you can't see the charts and data the briefer is looking at. (Unless, of course, you've made use of DUAT and the fax services: Note how using more than one source of information reinforces your knowledge.)

If you don't already do so, it's a good idea to use a standardized form to gather weather information. This can be of your own devising, or it can be one of the generic ones printed by the FAA. Regardless of where it comes from, a form will act as a checklist: If you fill in all the blanks, you'll know that you haven't forgotten to ask a critical question.

At a minimum, a form should have space for:
• **Synopsis -** This is the overall weather picture that will be the first thing the briefer reads to you. The worse the weather, the more complicated it will be, so plenty of space should be allowed for it.
• **Current and forecast conditions -** Room should be given for your

departure and destination airports, the alternate, and at least two or three reporting stations en route. The absolute minimum information you need is the time, ceiling, visibility, wind and altimeter.

• **Winds aloft** - The winds should be checked for several stations en route, and not only for your planned altitude but a few others as well.

• **Sigmets/Airmets** - These warnings, though critical, consist mostly of standard phrases and can be summarized in a few lines of text.

• **Cloud tops** - Often this information is not available, though it's very good to have. More than one pilot has slogged along in the clouds all the way to his destination, completely unaware that only 1,000 feet above is blue sky...because he forgot to ask.

• **Freezing level** - Obviously, this is more important in winter months. Again, space should be allotted for the departure, destination, alternate, and several other stations.

• **Radar summary** - Since this information is conveyed as radials and distances from reporting stations, it's often easier to visualize if you can sketch it on a chart. Many briefing sheets have small U.S. maps printed on them on which this can be sketched, but more useful is a larger map of your area of operations.

• **Nearest VFR** - This is not part of a standard briefing, but is a good thing to ask for. It will give you a clear idea of where to head if things go sour.

• **Pireps** - These are occasionally the most useful part of a briefing, but should always be taken with a grain of salt, especially when they're old. It's useful to have the pirep noted near the weather observation for its station.

• **Notams** - Again, it's useful to group notams near the affected facility's observation.

## Making the call

Armed with a briefing form, a chart opened to your route, and any other information you've gathered, it's time to call flight service and talk to the briefer.

The keys to a successful telephone briefing are understanding and cooperating with the briefing process. It's no secret that all briefings follow a standard format. Knowing the format allows you to concentrate on the information and ask questions to fill the gaps.

Every FSS briefing is tailored to your requirements, but the briefer needs basic information to do that. On initial contact, provide your pilot qualifications (private, commercial, instrument), type of flight (VFR or IFR), aircraft number or your name, the aircraft type, departure airport, route of flight, destination/alternate airport(s), probable cruising

---

## What type of briefing should you request?

- Standard: Complete briefing, assumes no previous information
- Abbreviated: Update recent briefing
- Outlook: Departure time more than six hours away
- In-flight: When ground briefing not possible

---

altitude(s), and estimated times of departure and en route. Don't give just a city name for your destination, provide the airport identifier, if known.

Next, ask for the briefing you need: standard, abbreviated or outlook. If you already have an overview from DUAT or other source, say so. The briefer will be reluctant to interpret DUAT or other computerized weather data. Most briefers don't mind the use of computerized weather and other automated weather services to get a general picture of conditions, but the briefer's job is to give a briefing from a vast database. So if you start by asking for this type of help, be prepared for an uncooperative briefer.

### Standard briefing

Ask for a standard briefing if you haven't had a previous briefing from an FSS or other source. The first three items covered in a standard briefing are: adverse conditions, synopsis, and, if warranted, the statement that VFR flight is not recommended. The briefer can combine or order these items any way he sees fit, depending on what he believes is the most logical presentation.

Adverse conditions are significant meteorological and aeronautical information that could cause a change in the route of flight, including hazardous weather conditions, e.g., thunderstorms, runway closures, navaid outages, etc. The synopsis is a brief statement describing the type, location and movement of weather systems and air masses over your route.

The briefer then covers the current conditions applicable to the flight using surface reports, pilot reports and radar reports. If the proposed time of departure is more than two hours away, the briefer will omit these items unless you ask for it.

The en route and destination forecasts follow. Conditions along the route are given in logical order: departure, climb, en route and descent. The destination forecast is given for the planned ETA, and any signifi-

---

## Give the briefer the following

- Your qualifications
- Type of flight (IFR or VFR)
- Aircraft number or your name
- Aircraft type
- Departure airport
- Route of flight
- Specific destination/alternate airport(s)
- Cruising altitude(s)
- Estimated time en route
- Estimated time of arrival

---

cant changes within one hour before and after the planned arrival are included.

Forecast winds aloft are given in knots and true north. The briefer will also interpolate wind direction and speed between levels and stations if needed.

## Notams

The briefer provides all available notams, which can include information on runway and/or airport closures and any other special activity at your destination, alterations to or closings of navaids along your route, and the like.

There are three types of notams: distant, local and Flight Data Center (FDC) notams. Distant notams are disseminated outside the area of the issuing FSS and usually cover large airports in metropolitan areas. Local notams are disseminated within the FSS service area and are issued for smaller fields outside metro areas. FDC Notams, which are regulatory in nature, are disseminated within 400 miles of the FSS. When published in the Class II Notams and the Airport/Facility Directory, distant and FDC notams aren't included in the briefing unless you ask. The notice is also removed from the FSS computers, so a check of these publications is important.

Once airborne, contact the destination FSS when in-range to check for local notams. Currently, airport and runway closures are listed as local notams, which aren't normally disseminated outside an FSS service area. There have been instances where pilots arriving at darkened airports discovered closed runways. There's a move under way to have all airport/runway closures listed as distant notams, which would ensure the information is disseminated over a wide area.

Lastly, any known ATC delays and flow control advisories that could affect the flight are given. At this point, you should ask for information regarding military training routes and MOA activity within 100 nautical miles of the FSS. For flights beyond 100 nm, ask an en route FSS. You can also ask for a review of the Class II Notams and A/FD publications, density altitude, information on air traffic services, customs/immigration procedures, ADIZ rules, Loran-C notams and any other assistance.

## Abbreviated briefing

Ask for this briefing if you obtained a computerized briefing or if you want to update a previous FSS briefing or if you only want two or three items.

Tell the briefer the source of the previous data and the time you received it, as well as the type of information needed. The briefer follows the same format as the standard briefing, except only choosing those items requested to update the information. If you only ask for two or three items, the briefer still advises on adverse conditions, present and forecast. Further details of those conditions are also provided at your request.

## Outlook briefing

Whenever your proposed departure time is six or more hours away, ask

---

### Briefing format

- Adverse conditions
- Synopsis
- VFR recommended/not recommended
- Current conditions
- En route forecast
- Destination forecast
- Winds aloft
- Notams
- Known ATC delays
- Other data as requested such as military training, MOA activity, review of notams, density altitude, air traffic rules, Loran-C notams.

for an outlook briefing and the briefer will provide all pertinent forecast data. Use this for planning only. Call an FSS closer to departure time to receive the current and updated forecast conditions, winds aloft, etc.

## In-flight briefing

When receiving a briefing on the ground is impossible or you simply need an en route update, contact FSS by radio and let them know what information is needed. They will follow the same format as discussed previously. The briefer may recommend switching to Flight Watch for weather advisories if conditions warrant.

Let the briefer finish giving all the information before asking questions or requesting additional information. This allows him to complete the sequence of items and lessens the chances that information will be left out of the briefing. Allow the briefer time to look through the data to pull out what he needs to give you. If you've spent any time looking at DUAT, you'll know that he's searching through pages of data.

## Pireps

One of the most valuable services you can perform for your fellow pilots is giving a pirep. FSS personnel use these to confirm forecast or current conditions and give everyone a picture of actual conditions. Giving pireps is particularly important during the icing season.

Tell an FSS the type aircraft you're flying, your position (either a distance from a VOR or a geographic point), your altitude, cloud cover and any other pertinent information such as turbulence or icing intensity. Use your own words, there is no special format for pireps. It also helps to report good conditions since forecasts are occasionally wrong.

If you don't have time to file a report with FSS, tell ATC to relay a report or wait until you've landed and call one in. Pireps remain in the system for two hours.

Thanks to DUAT and other services, the wait to speak to a briefer isn't as long as it used to be. Knowing the process can result in effortless briefing.

## On-line briefings

At the time of this book's publication, DUAT is still a free service provided by private companies under contract with FAA. Congress may cut funding for the program, but even if that happens it's unlikely it will disappear: it would probably become a pay-as-you-go service.

DUAT can be a powerful tool for the pilot, provided it's used with caution. Essentially, DUAT simply makes the exact same information a flight service specialist uses available directly to the pilot via a computer and modem. It's easy to get a whole raft of data displayed on your screen or printed out. You can have the service decode the "NWS-ese" and have the reports presented in more-or-less plain English.

However, just looking at the raw data is not the same as conferring with a trained FSS specialist. Unless you're a meteorologist, it's likely that the briefer has more weather training and knowledge than you do, and it's a good idea to pay attention to the voice of experience.

If the weather situation is fairly straightforward, a DUAT printout can stand on its own as your primary source of weather information. However, by and large the data gleaned from DUAT serves best when it's used as an adjunct to a live briefing.

DUAT can also provide a variety of charts, but compared to the ones produced by NOAA these aren't necessarily as useful.

The best source for NOAA charts, aside from a visit to the flight service station is via one of the weather fax services. For a nominal fee, you can get the exact same chart the briefer gets delivered to your fax machine in a matter of minutes.

These charts are excellent, and if you know how to interpret them can provide some of the best information a pilot can have. Again, it's better to ask the briefer unless you are *very* sure of yourself.

The weather fax services can also provide printouts of the standard NWS briefing products.

The bottom line with either DUAT or a weather fax service is that the pilot has to know just what to ask for and how to use it once he or she has got it. We'll cover the various NWS products and charts in detail in the next chapter.

# Tools of the Trade: Charts

No matter what style of briefing you prefer, whether it's based on a computer printout or a face-to-face meeting with the briefer, all are dependent on a collection of weather "products" produced by the National Weather Service (NWS) and the National Oceanographic and Atmospheric Administration (NOAA).

A pilot who relies entirely on live briefings doesn't actually need to know all of the products and their contents: for example, detailed knowledge of the various weather charts isn't taught much these days, because relatively few pilots have the opportunity to see one.

However, the more you know about the tools of the briefer's trade, the easier it will be for you to get a clear picture of the weather. And with the advent of DUAT and weather fax services, the same charts and reports used by flight service specialists are now easier for the average instrument pilot to get hold of than ever before.

Weather products come in two basic flavors: charts and reports. Both are complex, loaded with information, and virtually impossible to interpret without at least some training.

Two FAA publications that you should review if you haven't studied them recently are *Aviation Weather* (AC 00-6A) and *Aviation Weather Services* (AC 00-45C).

*Aviation Weather* is written in non-technical language and provides you with the essential information to understand the meteorological forces at work in the atmosphere. The companion publication, *Aviation Weather Services*, is updated periodically to reflect changes in weather products, services and capabilities. It explains how to interpret and use forecasts, weather maps, reports and prognostic charts.

*We'll deal with the two kinds of products separately. First up is a detailed discussion of weather charts; a look at reports and forecasts can be found in the next chapter.*

## Using charts

Most of the time, our weather briefings are conducted over the telephone and we rely heavily on what the briefer interprets for us. It's easy to forget what you don't use. Even those taking the instrument written exam, who should be up-to-date, have trouble with some of the finer points of weather chart interpretation.

It's not difficult to interpret weather chart data. The blackened-in station identifiers, arrow-like barbs, dots and dashed lines all have logical meanings. Make an effort to memorize the symbols you need and carry a reminder chart or ask weather briefing personnel about the rest.

The two charts that are absolutely essential for planning any flight are the weather depiction chart and the radar summary chart. The other charts produced by the National Weather Service include: the significant weather prognostic, surface analysis, winds and temperatures aloft, composite moisture stability, severe weather outlook, constant pressure and tropopause data charts. All of these supply vital weather information as well, but the two most important are the depiction and radar summary.

Think of these first two charts as building blocks, or better yet, pieces of a jigsaw puzzle. Each chart represents another part of the overall weather picture. Put them together and you'll have as complete an idea as possible of what the weather is doing and where it's going.

Both the weather depiction and radar summary charts work in concert with each other. Some pilots prefer to review the radar summary first, noting where the heavy-duty returns are located, then go to the weather depiction to see the location of IFR weather. It really doesn't matter which order you read them, as long as you use both together for that first look at the weather.

## Weather Depiction

Let's discuss the weather depiction chart first, which provides basic information in a somewhat pictorial fashion, and in less detail than the surface analysis chart, in order for you to see the overall weather picture at a glance. This information includes: heights of cloud bases, present weather and obstructions to vision, visibilities, as well as contoured areas of cloud and weather coverage, which indicate IFR, MVFR, and VFR weather. It may also show features such as major fronts and high

# Weather chart summary

• **Weather Depiction** - Surface observations are used by the computer to produce this chart every three hours to depict areas of IFR (ceilings less than 1000 feet and/or visibility less than three miles), MVFR (ceilings 1000-3000 feet and/or visibility 3-5 miles) and VFR (ceilings greater than 3000 feet and visibility greater than five miles).

• **Radar Summary** - Updated hourly, this chart shows precipitation echoes, tops and bases, intensity and intensity trends. It does not detect clouds and fog. Precipitation intensity levels are shown from Level 1 (weak) to Level 6 (extreme).

• **Surface Analysis** - Produced every three hours, this chart shows the location of fronts and pressure systems.

• **Significant Weather Prog** - For planning purposes, these charts show forecasts of ceilings, visibilities, turbulence, precipitation, fronts, air masses and freezing levels. A 12 and 24 hour significant weather prog for the surface to 24,000 feet is produced every six hours. A 36 and 48 hour surface map of the synoptic situation is produced twice daily.

• **Composite Moisture Stability** - There are four panels to this chart: stability (to review the potential for convective activity), freezing level (reveals areas of possible icing), average relative humidity (to determine areas of clouds and precipitation) and precipitable water (not as useful to pilots as other three, but does show amount of precipitable water on any given day).

• **Severe Weather Outlook (AC)** - Shows areas of possible thunderstorm activity and severe thunderstorms for 12 and 24 hour period. Good for advance planning.

Other charts of interest:

• **Forecast Winds and Temperatures Aloft (FD)** - Produced twice daily, these charts range from 3000 feet agl to 39,000 feet msl. Temperatures are shown for 6000 feet and above.

• **Constant Pressure Analysis** - Prepared twice daily, these charts depict upper air weather patterns that may differ significantly from the surface charts. Five charts are produced for the following altitudes: 850 millibars (5000 feet), 700 millibars (10,000), 500 millibars (18,000 feet), 300 millibars (30,000 feet) and 200 millibars (39,000 feet).

and low pressure centers. Using the depiction chart, it's possible to note at a glance if you can expect IFR or VFR flight, whether it will be cloudy, and so forth.

The data used to compile weather depiction charts are taken from the surface analysis observations made during the preceding hour, hence the similarity in symbols between this chart and the surface analysis chart. The charts are issued eight times a day at three-hour intervals, so you should remember that this is not current weather data. The information on these charts can be up to four hours old by the time you see it. They also cannot show variations in the weather and terrain between reporting stations, making the en route weather picture incomplete.

The symbols used on the weather depiction chart are probably the easiest to memorize. There are seven symbols relating to percentage of sky cover and one symbol, unique to the weather depiction chart, that denotes clouds topping ridges.

There's a number typed under each station symbol on the depiction chart. This is the cloud height, in hundreds of feet, above ground level. If the clouds are few or scattered, this height is the lowest layer. If the clouds are broken or greater, this height is the ceiling. A station circle with a broken or greater symbol without the height number means a thin sky cover.

A partially to totally obscured sky is indicated with an x in the station circle. When a partially obscured sky without clouds is observed, there will be no height entry; and if a cloud layer is present, an entry will be present on the chart. The height entry under a total obscuration symbol means vertical visibility into the obscuration instead of ceiling height.

Precipitation (present weather) and obstructions to vision are indicated with symbols which appear to the left of the station circle. When several different types of weather occur at the station, only the most significant is depicted on the chart.

Visibility, when it is six miles or less, is listed in statute miles and fractions of miles and also appears to the left of the weather symbol.

The contoured areas on the chart that are shaded indicate IFR, with ceilings less than 1,000 feet and/or visibility less than three miles. Contoured areas without shading are MVFR (marginal VFR), with ceilings 1,000 feet to 3,000 feet (inclusive) and/or visibility three to five miles (inclusive). VFR areas, with ceiling greater than 3,000 feet or unlimited and visibility greater than five miles, are not outlined. These three categories are also explained on the lower right corner of the chart, just in case you need a reminder.

Other features that may appear on the chart are the position of fronts and high and low pressure areas. The last two numbers of the sea level pressure (in millibars) is often indicated on the chart near the high or low pressure symbol.

For example, if you see an underlined 08, you know that the sea level pressure is 1008 millibars at that location.

One other feature that only appears at six-hour intervals is a tide deviation entry along the Atlantic and Pacific coastlines. This is given when the tide height departs from the predicted normal height. The difference between these two figures is given in tens, units, and tenths of feet. For example, +020 means the tide is 2.0 feet higher than the predicted normal.

## Radar Summary

Next, you need to review the radar summary chart. This chart displays areas of radar returns produced either by liquid or frozen water droplets of precipitation size. The data is collected from various radar sites each hour and is transmitted to a central computer to produce the composite chart. The chart is transmitted to National Weather Service offices and flight service stations on an hourly basis, for a total of 17 times in a 24-hour period.

Radar echoes are classified into six levels of intensity: 1—weak, 2—moderate, 3—strong, 4—very strong, 5—intense, and 6—extreme. These levels are further grouped into three categories, levels 1 and 2, levels 3 and 4, and levels 5 and 6.

When precipitation echoes are plotted on the chart, what results looks like a topographic, or contour map. Looking at the precipitation echo contours on the radar summary chart and comparing them to the locations of fronts, IFR conditions and degree of cloud cover found on the depiction chart gives you a good overall view of what the weather was doing at the time the charts were prepared.

Precipitation levels are not plotted since the reported echoes already indicate levels of intensity. You should assume that any area where echoes are depicted as very strong, for example, will have precipitation falling at a very heavy rate. When in doubt, use the maximum possible intensity when trying to determine an intensity level from the chart.

Intensity trends are indicated by a (-) decreasing, (+) increasing, or no symbol if remaining unchanged, and are plotted beside the precipitation type. If you see a symbol for frozen precipitation, e.g., the symbol for snow—S, followed by a plus sign, it does not refer to the intensity trend, but to the fact that this is a newly reported area of precipitation. Actual intensities for frozen precipitation cannot be determined from the contour lines because these lines correlate only to liquid precipitation.

A heavy line through a contoured area indicates a line of thunderstorms. The abbreviation SLD next to it means that the thunderstorm line is solid (8/10ths coverage or more). Actual areas of hail are shown by a line connecting the word HAIL to a small filled-in square.

## Top and base data

Maximum echo tops and bases (when the data are available) are shown connected to small filled-in squares, which depict the actual locations. The heights of the echo tops and bases are given in hundreds of feet msl. The tops reported are the highest in that area. Absence of base data indicates that the base is at the surface, but keep in mind that precipitation usually reaches the surface; tops are easier to spot on radar. If you see base data that is a few thousand feet above the surface, you may want to look at it a bit more closely as the precipitation may be evaporating before it reaches the ground.

Top and base data are entered as three-digit numbers above and below a short line connected to the location square. Remember that top data should be considered approximate. Radar can only detect the tops of precipitation, not actual cloud tops. In areas of the country not served by National Weather Service radar, the information used for top data is either from pilot reports and indicates actual cloud tops or is nonexistent (such as in the western U.S.) due to lack of radar coverage.

Movement of individual cells within a line or in an area can be different from the rest of the line or area. Specific symbols are used to distinguish this difference in movement. Individual cell movement is indicated by an arrow, with the speed in knots entered next to it. Whole line or area movement is noted by a shaft and barb combination. The shaft indicates the direction and the barb indicates the speed. A half barb is five knots, a whole barb is ten knots, and a pennant is fifty knots. Little movement is indicated by the abbreviation LM.

Severe weather watch areas also can be found on the radar summary chart. They are outlined by heavy dashed lines, often in the form of a rectangular box, and are divided into two types. The first is tornado watches and the second is severe thunderstorm watches. The type of watch and the watch number are noted inside of the box, as close to the northeast corner of the box as possible. For example, a WS400 means a severe thunderstorm watch, and it is the 400th such watch issued that year. The watch number will also be printed at the bottom of the chart along with the valid until time and the issuance time.

## Canadian radar data

Interpreting radar data from Canadian sites is similar to reading the

U.S. chart. Area, line, cell movements and precipitation types, intensity and intensity trends all mean the same as U.S. data. On U.S. charts, the echo top reports are converted from meters to feet msl. Where it can get a bit confusing is when both Canadian and U.S. data are plotted together. If you see a box that appears to be a severe weather watch box located in Canada near the border, look again. Remember that U.S. watch boxes are outlined in heavy dashed lines, not solid lines. Canadian radar plots are often outlined in light solid lines and carry an identifier inside the box.

## No clouds or fog

When using the radar summary chart, remember that the radar detects only liquid or frozen droplets of precipitation size. It cannot detect smaller droplets, such as those found in clouds and fog. The absence of echoes does not guarantee that the air is free of weather and clouds. The actual cloud tops may be higher than the echo tops, since the echo tops are plotted from returns of falling precipitation.

You should always note the location and movement of lines of thunderstorms, especially if your route takes you near them. Penetration of a line depends on your understanding of the conditions and the use of airborne weather radar. If you aren't properly equipped, plan to deviate or wait it out on the ground. Areas of widely scattered thunderstorms, such as those common in Florida, can often be circumnavigated visually. Be sure to check for areas of missing radar reports (NA or OM) before you assume it's safe to fly through that area. Otherwise, you might find an unpleasant surprise waiting for you.

You can encounter conflicting data on the chart, such as when one area of precipitation is reported by two separate radar sites. The data will be slightly different due to the variations in perspective and distance of the radar sites from the echoes. When in doubt, use the data showing the most hazardous conditions.

## Surface Analysis and Significant Weather Prog

The radar summary and weather depiction charts taken together can give you the big picture when starting a weather briefing. However, that picture lacks real detail, and it's already getting old by the time you see it. The next series of charts to review are the surface analysis and significant weather prognostic charts.

The surface analysis chart, also known as the surface weather chart, can be intimidating due to an abundance of detailed data. Don't let this stop you from using it. This chart provides valuable information on the locations of fronts and pressure systems, wind direction and speed, types of clouds and precipitation, temperature and dew point.

The data for the surface analysis chart is collected, plotted and transmitted by computer to all weather reporting stations every three hours. When used in conjunction with other charts, particularly the weather depiction, radar summary, and prognostic charts, an accurate overview of weather trends is available to you. Patience and some memorization is required to interpret each piece of data on the chart.

Many of the symbols on the surface analysis chart should be familiar: the H and L symbols for high and low pressure systems, the isobar lines that depict the sea level pressure pattern, the strings of pointed and rounded pips depicting the types and locations of fronts, and the total sky cover symbols for each reporting station (which are the same as found on the weather depiction chart).

You may have forgotten how to interpret some of the depicted data since the instrument written exam, so let's review first that data which surrounds each of the reporting stations.

## Station symbols

The station symbol is a small circle that is darkened, depending on the amount of cloud cover over the station. There are seven categories of sky cover, depicted by symbols that are easy to remember, ranging from a clear circle (indicating a clear sky) to a circle containing a small x (for sky totally or partially obscured).

Extending from the station circle is an arrow-like barb that depicts wind direction and speed. Wind direction is indicated by the shaft of the arrow, which depicts the direction from which the wind is blowing. The feathers depict wind speed and are used in various combinations; a half-flag equals five knots, a full flag equals ten knots, and a pennant equals fifty knots. An outer circle drawn around a station indicates calm wind.

The data at the twelve o'clock position above the station circle depicts the type of high-level and mid-level clouds, and directly at the six o'clock position you'll find the symbol for the type of low-level cloud observed over the station. (A complete list of symbols used to distinguish cloud types is contained in *Aviation Weather Services*, AC 00-45C. You may wish to remember the more commonly used ones and copy the page as a reference.)

Proceeding in a clockwise manner, the next bit of data indicates the atmospheric pressure. This is given in millibars and is shown on the chart as a three-digit number (to the nearest tenth of a millibar). For a millibar reading that is 1000 or greater, add the prefix 10 to the three digits and for less than 1000, add a 9 to determine the correct figure. For example, if you see plotted data of 225, you know this is 1022.5 millibars, whereas a plotted reading of 951 will convert to 995.1 millibars. (Sea level pressure is 1013.2 millibars.)

Below the millibar data are numbers and a symbol that indicate by how much, in tenths of a millibar, the reading has changed and its general tendency (moving upward, downward, steady, or a combination thereof). This trend will give you a clue as to how rapidly (or slowly) the pressure system over the station is moving in or away and will indicate what type of weather to expect. Once again, a listing of these symbols is contained *Aviation Weather Services*.

The next bit of data is the amount of precipitation that fell at the station in the last six hours. This is given in the nearest hundredths of an inch. Moving further clockwise to the seven o'clock position, is the dew point in degrees Fahrenheit, and then the symbol for the present weather, which can include precipitation, sky obscuration, or active storms over the station.

Last, the current temperature in degrees Fahrenheit is given. When compared with the dew point, you can determine the likelihood that fog will form or, in the winter, whether ice will be in the clouds. Remember that the closer together the two temperatures, the more possibility that these phenomena will occur.

## Frontal activity

The surface analysis chart also provides information regarding frontal activity. In addition to the depiction of warm and cold fronts, there is numeric information that specifies frontal intensity.

There are 12 classifications for frontal activity, depending on the type and maturity of the front and whether it is located aloft or at the surface. Colors are also applied to these symbols by weather station personnel for ease in identification. (Red is used for warm fronts and blue for cold fronts).

Fronts are also coded as to type, intensity, and character. This code is a three-digit number that appears next to the front, somewhere along its length. The first digit gives the type of front, ranging from zero to 9, with zero as a quasi-stationary front at the surface and 9 as a convergence line. The numbers you will most likely see are 2 and 3 for warm front at the surface and aloft, 4 and 5 for cold front at the surface and aloft, and 6 for an occlusion.

The next digit denotes the intensity of the front, ranging from zero for no specification, to 9 for strong and increasing. Categories 1, 2, and 3 are applied to weak fronts; 4, 5, and 6 are moderate in intensity; and 7, 8, and 9 are strong fronts.

The last digit is the character of the front, with zero as no specification, to 9 as position doubtful. The ones we're mostly like to see are 1 for frontal area activity decreasing, 2 for frontal area activity with little change, and 3 for frontal area activity increasing.

We can illustrate the meaning of the combined code with an example. If a front has 463 next to it, we can interpret this to mean a cold front at the surface that is moderate in intensity but increasing in strength and is also increasing in types of activity associated with it (e.g., thunderstorms). (Again, a complete listing of the codes are contained in *Aviation Weather Services*.)

## Prog Charts

The next series of charts should be consulted after you have looked over the surface analysis chart. These are the significant weather prognostic, or prog, charts. They come in the low-level and high-level varieties, but we'll discuss the low-level ones, which depict forecast data below 24,000 feet (the high-level progs extend from 24,000 feet to 63,000 feet).

The low-level significant weather progs are presented on four panels and are issued four times each day with valid times—the times at which the charted forecast at any particular location is expected to exist. These times are 0000Z, 0600Z, 1200Z, 1800Z. Due to the time required to prepare the chart, the information is valid for only 6 hours after the receipt of the 12-hour panel. To determine forecast conditions after 6 hours, you'll need to interpolate the data between the 12- and 24-hour panels.

The two lower panels are surface progs and are issued as 12-hour and 24-hour forecasts respectively, valid as of the time noted on the chart. The two upper panels are progs for significant weather forecast to occur from the surface to the 400 millibar (24,000 feet) level in the same 12-hour and 24-hour periods, also valid as of the time noted.

The symbols used on the surface progs are those you're used to seeing, high and low markings and the various depictions for the fronts. Pressure center movement is shown by an arrow, which indicates the direction of movement, and a number that indicates the speed of that movement in knots. Sometimes, isobars showing the forecast location of the pressure systems are also included in the 24-hour panel.

The surface progs also depict areas of forecast precipitation and/or thunderstorms by enclosing these areas either with a smooth line, which indicates areas of expected continuous or intermittent (stable) precipitation, or with a dashed and dot line, which indicates areas of showers and/or thunderstorms, as well as areas of continuous or intermittent precip with embedded thunderstorms and showers.

The symbols for the various types of precipitation and the intensity of that precip are the same ones you'll often see on television weather: a dot for rain, a snowflake for snow, a dot with a tail (comma) for drizzle, and so on. A single symbol will appear for intermittent precip, and a double symbol for continuous precip. If the precipitation affects half or more of one area, the area will be shaded.

The significant weather prog panels (the upper ones) depict IFR, MVFR, turbulence and freezing levels. (The legend for the symbols used in these areas is provided at the center of each prog chart.) Areas of forecast IFR weather are enclosed with smooth lines. A scalloped line encloses areas of MVFR, and VFR areas are not outlined. Keep in mind this is not the manner in which IFR and MVFR weather is depicted on the weather depiction chart.

Many pilots need to review the symbols for turbulence on the prog charts. It is an often-missed question on FAA written exams. Areas of moderate or greater turbulence are enclosed by a long-dashed line. The FAA and NWS assume you know that areas of thunderstorms will have moderate or greater turbulence, so these are not depicted.

The symbol inserted in the center of this marked area indicates the intensity of turbulence, with the expected base and top of the turbulence layer given in hundreds of feet msl and depicted as numbers inserted and below a short line. (The symbol for moderate turbulence itself looks like a pointed hat, and severe turbulence is depicted by a double pointed hat. Don't be confused by this symbol, it just stands for the word turbulence. The point on the hat does not indicate direction.)

No number above the line means the turbulence extends above the upper limit of the chart (24,000 feet). One example of this notation might be 060 with a short line above it, which means the turbulence starts at 6000 feet and extends to 24,000 feet. Turbulence forecast from the surface to above 24,000 feet is noted by SFC below the line with the upper number left blank. If it's from the surface to 20,000 feet, the bottom notation will be SFC and the upper, above the line, will be 200.

Finally, freezing level information is displayed on the panels with contours for the highest level drawn at 4,000-foot intervals and labeled in hundreds of feet msl. These contours are drawn with a short-dashed line. A freezing level at the surface is depicted with a dotted line and labeled SFC or 32F. Remember that the chart does not outline areas of forecast icing. You can take for granted that icing is implied in precip and clouds above the freezing level.

A 36-hour and 48-hour prog chart is also issued, and the depiction of data on these panels is the same except that no freezing precipitation is noted; scalloped lines denote areas of overcast clouds with no reference to cloud bases. A brief discussion is included at the bottom of the chart that gives the forecaster's explanation of the forecast for the entire 12- to 48-hour period.

The prog charts enable you to avoid areas of forecast turbulence and icing, but remember that these are only forecasts and do not reflect actual conditions. By using these charts in conjunction with the surface analysis, which gives you the most current weather, and the weather depiction and radar summary charts, you will have a much clearer picture of the weather, helping you to plan a safer flight.

## Composite Moisture Stability

Knowing where moisture is located and its movement can be a key factor in determining your route of flight, or even if you should go at all. The composite moisture stability chart provides valuable information on the potential development of clouds and precipitation.

This chart is actually four charts in one, with the data on each panel updated twice daily (valid times are 1200 and 0000 UTC). Included on the chart are: the air stability panel, the freezing level panel, the precipitable water panel and the average relative humidity panel. Reporting stations are indicated on each panel by a distinctive symbol keyed to the availability of upper air data. (The legend for these station symbols are on the precipitable water panel.)

The pressure altitudes at which observations are made begin at the surface and move upward to 1000 millibars (3000 feet), 850 millibars (5000 feet), 700 millibars (10,000 feet), and 500 millibars (18,000 feet). Levels between the mandatory levels where significant changes in temperature and/or moisture are observed are appropriately called significant levels.

The air stability panel is the upper left panel of the chart. Only two values appear above each station: the lifted index (top figure) and the K index (bottom figure).

## Lifted index

The lifted index indicates the stability of the air. The number is deter- mined by computing the temperature of a parcel of air as if it is lifted to a pressure altitude of 500 millibars. This temperature is then subtracted from the actual temperature observed at the 500 millibar level (approxi- mately 18,000 feet msl) to result in a positive, negative, or zero figure.

A positive index indicates stable air, with very high values (10 and above) indicating extremely stable air. A negative figure means the air is unstable and is likely to be convective in nature, and a high negative value indicates extreme conditions. A zero index indicates that the air is neutrally stable, that is, neither stable or unstable. (On the panel, the station symbol is blackened for a zero or negative index. A solid line connects values of four or less in increments of four.)

The lifted index has a few precautions to keep in mind. When the index is computed, it is assumed that the air near the surface will be lifted to the 500 millibar level, but this doesn't always occur in the real world. A high negative value is possible when no convective activity is present if the air is not lifted high enough to develop into cells.

It is best to use the index as an indication of thunderstorm severity, instead of the probability of development. (This is why it makes sense to cross-check the other weather charts which show current and forecast conditions.)

The lifted index is also susceptible to surface heating, which makes the value less stable (less positive). This shows up more in the 0000Z observation period, as the ground is heated by the sun.

## K index

The K index, used mostly by meteorologists, is computed with a more complex formula using temperatures and dew points from various millibar levels. It is not an index of true stability, so you should use it only to supplement the other weather information already available. A high K index during warmer months indicates conditions that are conducive to air mass thunderstorm formation (as opposed to the frontal variety, where the reliability of the K index decreases).

In cold months, the K index is skewed as a result of cold temperatures and lack of moisture, making high values invalid for use in predicting thunderstorm activity. In addition, K index values can be skewed in mountainous areas due to variations in air flow over terrain.

When using the stability panel to determine types of clouds and possible precipitation, remember that stable air supports stratiform clouds and steady precipitation, and unstable air allows convective clouds and showery precipitation to develop. For example, in the winter you could deduce from the panel that areas of stable air, which allow stratiform to develop, might be areas of extensive icing.

Conversely, in the summer, indications of highly unstable air might be areas to expect convective activity, turbulence and thunderstorms. Remember, an unstable index does not always mean thunderstorms are certain to develop.

## Freezing level

On the lower left of the chart, you'll find the one panel that demands special attention in the winter: the freezing level. Solid line contours are drawn to indicate each level of freezing temperatures, starting with the lowest observed level and moving upward in 4000-foot intervals. (This differs from the low-level significant weather prognostic chart, which indicates the highest forecast freezing level.) Each level is marked in hundreds of feet msl. Areas enclosed by a dashed line are groups of stations reporting the 32 degree F isotherm at the surface. The notation BF (for below freezing) will also appear within or near the enclosed area. (An M means data is missing for that station.)

Interpreting the observed data is not difficult with practice. Most stations report only the height of the lowest freezing level, but you'll note others with several numbers stacked in a column over the station. This indicates that several different freezing levels, separated by levels above freezing, are present. Read the numbers from the bottom up, since the lowest freezing level will always appear in that position.

For example, you might see 35, 43, and 93, with 35 as the bottom number. This means the lowest freezing level is 3500 feet msl. It is below freezing from 3500 feet to 4300 feet, above freezing from 4300 feet to 9300 feet, below freezing from 9300 feet upward. In another example, if the notation BF appears as the bottom number with the number 25 then 100, it is below freezing from the surface to 2500 feet, above freezing from 2500 feet to 10,000 feet, then below freezing above 10,000 feet.

These multiple entries should send up a warning flag which says POSSIBLE ICING, especially when the stations are reporting some form of precipitation. Precipitation falling through the various layers of above and below freezing temperatures is an ugly outlook for any flight through that area.

## Vapor content

The precipitable water panel appears on the upper right of the chart. This panel analyzes the water vapor content of the air from the surface to the 500 millibar level. The final computed value for each station is the amount of liquid water, in the form of precipitation, that would be present in the air if the water vapor condensed.

The data that appears beside each station is the amount of computed precipitable water (to the nearest hundredths of an inch), which appears above a short line, with the percent of normal value (the amount of precipitable water actually present compared to what is normally expected) for the month appearing below the line. For example, Los Angeles, California, might indicate .32/55, which means 32 hundredths of an inch of precipitable water is present in the air, which is 55% of normal (below normal) for any day of that month.

Light and heavy solid contour lines (called isopleths) are drawn and labeled for every 0.25 inch and 0.50 inch intervals, respectively. Station symbols that are blackened depict precipitable water values of 1.00 inch or more. (An M appearing above the line means the data is missing. Missing values below the line indicate there was insufficient data available to compute the percentage.) Although the main use of this panel is to determine the likelihood of flash floods on the ground, you can use it to spot long-term trends in the increase or decrease in amounts of water vapor present in the atmosphere along your route of flight.

## Relative humidity

The panel on the lower right portion of the chart plots average relative humidity data observed from the surface to the 500 millibar level. This value is plotted as a percentage. Station symbols are blackened to indicate humidities of 50 percent or greater. Light contour lines (called isohumes in this panel) are drawn in 10 percent increments, with heavy lines indicating values of 10, 50 and 90 percent.

This panel can be used to determine the amount of air saturation over any given area. Humidities of 70 percent or higher indicate possible cloudiness and precipitation. In the summer, you might deduce that the more saturated air may also be unstable, with showers or thunderstorms a likely result. In the winter, it can alert you to frozen precipitation. However, when looking at both the precipitable water panel and this one, it is important for you to remember that high humidity values do not also mean correspondingly high water vapor values.

Once you've completed a detailed review of each panel, take a minute to pull the information together. You should be able to determine the stability of a weather system, its moisture content and the possible hazards it can produce as a result. As the system moves, it will usually carry these characteristics with it, so you are reasonably safe in extrapolating forward from the chart issue time.

## Severe Weather Outlook

The severe weather outlook (AC) chart is a forecast of expected extreme conditions. It is produced manually once a day (as opposed to the computer-generated twice a day composite moisture stability chart) and gives a 24-hour outlook for thunderstorm activity. The chart has two panels: the one on the left covers the 12-hour period between 1200Z and 0000Z and the one on the right covers the period between 0000Z and 1200Z .

Areas of possible thunderstorm activity are indicated with a line tipped with an arrowhead. If you face the direction in which the arrowhead points, you can expect the thunderstorm activity to the right of the line. The notation APCHG depicts an area of activity that may intensify to the severe category, meaning that winds greater than or equal to 35 knots but less than 50 knots and/or hail greater than or equal to 1/2 inch but less that 3/4 inch in diameter are expected.

Areas of expected severe thunderstorm activity are outlined and single-hatched. These single-hatched areas may be categorized as slight risk, moderate risk, or high risk and define the likelihood of severe weather development. Tornado watches are only plotted on the chart if one is in effect at the time the chart is drawn. This watch area is cross-hatched. Again, remember that this chart is for planning purposes only. It does not provide you with actual observed data, but only alerts you to areas of possible severe weather development so you can flight plan accordingly.

Both the composite moisture stability chart and the severe weather outlook chart have unique stories to tell. The composite moisture stability chart reveals the inner character of a weather system. From it you can deduce how wet or dry the system is, its overall stability, and what types of clouds and precipitation to expect as a result. The severe weather outlook chart provides an uncluttered look at the forecast areas of extremely dangerous weather. Both charts, when used in conjunction with the others, strengthen the image of the weather picture in your mind.

## The toolbox

There's a lot to absorb on these charts, and it takes a lot of training and experience to use them effectively. Again, we encourage you to rely on the briefer's knowledge when using them.

However, checking the charts yourself, especially when the weather is unsettled, can provide not only greater insight into the workings of weather, but a better feeling for what you'll be facing once aloft.

# Tools of the Trade: Reports

In this chapter we take a highly detailed look at some of the more troublesome reports and other phenomena lurking in the bowels of the National Weather Service computers.

All instrument pilots are familiar with the various basic types of weather observation: terminal forecasts, area forecasts, pireps and surface reports. By and large these reports are known quantities, but there's one thing about them that gives many pilots fits: the abbreviations used in them.

In the first part of this chapter, we'll take a look at some of the abbreviations you're likely to find on a typical NWS printout.

## Watch Those Remarks

What are RADAT, BINOVC and D5? If you guessed the latest aircraft radar system, video game or dandruff shampoo, you're wrong. These are just three of hundreds of contractions that can be found in the remarks section of an hourly surface observation report.

Before you yawn, think about this: the most important information in an observation can be the remarks, which can alert you to changing conditions that you might not notice from the observation itself.

Remarks are used to expand or amplify data already reported; describe observed, but not presently occurring, conditions at the weather reporting station; or report other significant information, such as runway visibility and runway visual range, hazardous cloud types and freezing level.

When used, remarks appear as the last item in the hourly report and follow the altimeter setting. The standard aviation weather contractions used can be found in *Aviation Weather Services*, AC00-45C. Some

---

## Selected report types

• **Surface Aviation Weather Reports (SA)** - These are the familiar hourly and special sequences of observations that provide ceiling, visibility, etc., as well as any pertinent remarks.

• **Pireps (UA)** - These are much more valuable to forecasters and briefers than pilots sometimes believe. Pireps are used to fill in the gaps between reporting stations and are used to develop and amend forecasts.

• **Terminal Forecast (FT)** - These are for airports and include an area within five nm of the runway complex. Issued three times daily, they consist of an 18-hour forecast plus a six-hour outlook.

• **Domestic Area Forecast (FA)** - Issued three times daily, this forecast covers general conditions for several states. Each FA is a 12-hour forecast plus a six-hour outlook. It gives an overall picture of what to expect and includes: hazards/flight precautions, synopsis, icing, turbulence, low-level wind shear, significant clouds and weather.

• **Radar Report (SD)** - Issued at 35 past each hour, with special reports issued as conditions warrant. The observations are from both NWS and ATC radar sites around the country. These observations are also used to generate the radar summary chart.

---

remarks are routinely reported, while others are at the discretion of the observer.

## Visibility

The first routine remark is, when applicable, runway visibility or runway visual range. Runway visibility (RVV) is visibility from a location along a specified runway and is reported in miles and fractions of a mile. Runway visual range (RVR), on the other hand, is the maximum horizontal distance down a specified instrument runway at which a pilot can see and identify standard high intensity runway lights. It's reported in hundreds of feet.

Both RVV and RVR are surface measurements, not slant range visibilities. As a result, the minimum visibility required for landing might be present on the ground, but not at MDA or DH.

Their appearance depends on several criteria: RVV must be less than two miles or the prevailing visibility less than approach minimums; RVR must be 6000 feet or less, or prevailing visibility one mile or less; and the observations for both must be made continuously. Some stations using equipment that give instantaneous observations may not transmit the visibility values because these values change too rapidly.

RVV and RVR reports are a series of letters and numbers, starting with the runway designator and then the contraction VV or VR, followed by the visibility or visual range. Both RVV and RVR are reported for a 10-minute period preceding the observation time. Variable readings taken during the 10-minute period are separated by the letter V. If the visual range or visibility remains relatively unchanged throughout one 10-minute period, a single value is sent, indicating that the value is constant.

Other remarks may elaborate on the visibility reported at the beginning of the observation with a separate surface or tower visibility. These additional visibilities alert you to variable conditions within the airport environment itself that could be critical during landing or takeoff.

The following are examples of additional visibility reports: **X 1/ 4VF.../SFC VSBY 1/4V1/2 THN F NW** decoded means sky obscured, prevailing visibility one quarter variable in fog...surface visibility variable between one-quarter and one-half mile, thin fog northwest (possible clearing coming from that direction). **CLR 25.../TWR VSBY 1/4 F W** means clear, prevailing visibility 25 miles...tower visibility one quarter, fog west (as a fog bank rolls over the tower).

## Hazardous cloud types

Routine remarks often describe cloud types that are highly significant and usually hazardous. Pay close attention if any of the following abbreviations appear.

• **Towering cumulus (TCU)** indicates that the lower atmosphere is unstable and conducive to thunderstorm development. Related hazards include turbulence and wind shear.

• **Cumulonimbus (CB)**, full-blown thunderstorms, contain a mixed bag of aviation hazards: turbulence, icing, hail and wind shear.

• **Altocumulus Castellanus (ACCAS)** is a mid-level cloud and indicates moist, unstable conditions aloft, but not necessarily below the base of the cloud. These clouds may appear above stable surface inversions and can indicate thunderstorm development.

• **Cumulonimbus Mamma (CBMAM)** are characteristic of violent up- and down-drafts and are often associated with severe weather, such as

a squall line. Expect severe or greater turbulence, among other hazards.
• **Standing lenticular altocumulus (ACSL)** and standing lenticular cirrocumulus (CCSL) are upper air clouds characteristic of standing or mountain wave conditions. The term ROTOR CLD may also appear in the report. Wave conditions develop when 40-knot or greater winds blow perpendicular to a mountain or ridge line. Strong updrafts and downdrafts, up to 3000 feet per minute, are common several hundred miles downstream of the mountain or ridge and conditions can extend from the ground to over 30,000 feet.
• **Virga** is falling precipitation that evaporates below the cloud before hitting the ground. Strong wind shear turbulence can develop in the vicinity of virga as the air is cooled by the falling precipitation.

Other cloud types that may routinely appear are roll, wall and shelf clouds, all of which can indicate convective activity, thunderstorms or severe weather.

Additionally, the msl heights of bases and tops of sky cover layers can be included. This information comes directly from pilot reports, and is omitted if it's more than 15 minutes old unless deemed significant by the reporting station.

## Freezing level and icing

RADAT, the contraction for freezing level information, appears in the 00Z and 12Z reports from stations taking upper air observations. These stations are listed in the U.S. government Airport/Facility Directory. The data reports the freezing level in hundreds of feet msl and the relative humidity at that level. High relative humidity indicates abundant moisture and a strong possibility of icing in clouds at and above the freezing level. Multiple freezing levels are also reported.

The coded report begins with RADAT, followed by the relative humidity at the freezing level. When more than one level is observed, the highest relative humidity observed is reported. Next is the letter, L, M or H, which indicates that the relative humidity is for the lowest, middle or highest level.

Following this is the msl height at which the upper air sounding crossed the freezing level. Heights appear as three-digit numbers, for example: 024 is 2400 feet or 110 is 11,000 feet. No more than three levels are coded and transmitted. If the 0-degree C isotherm is crossed by the sounding more than three times, the levels coded are the lowest and the top two levels. If applicable, a number following a slash mark at the end of the report indicates the additional number of crossings of the 0-degree C isotherm.

Occasionally, the station observer detects ice at certain altitudes. In this case, the data is entered as RAICG to indicate that icing data follows, then the height at which the icing occurred.

## Other Remarks

Additional items that may be included in remarks are further elaborations of sky and ceiling conditions, obscuring phenomena such as fog or smoke, weather and obstruction to vision, wind and pressure, all of which can give you additional information on changing conditions.

Many remarks include locations of the particular weather phenomena in relation to the station. The observer always starts from true north, then moves clockwise around the station. For example, a report of **RDGS OBSCD E S-N**, means ridges obscured east and south through north. If your route lies in one of those directions, you can determine a safer route around or through the weather.

Many of these remarks are at the discretion of the observer, who can occasionally confuse you with ambiguous or unnecessary elaboration. Some observers use highly technical or local terms to describe conditions that can be easily translated into universally understood weather contractions, while others can make mistakes in correctly reporting the data, causing errors in logic between the observations and the remarks. If in doubt, call a flight service station to clarify the remark.

## Hazards can still exist

Also remember that the absence of remarks doesn't indicate the absence of hazardous weather. Just because the observer ignored the cumulonimbus mamma over the station doesn't mean it isn't there. Be alert to other parts of the briefing that indicate hazardous conditions.

If you haven't guessed by now, the abbreviations RADAT, BINOVC and D5 are, respectively, freezing level data, breaks in the overcast, and dust obscuring 5/10ths of the sky. If your memory was a little fuzzy, it's time to review.

*Next up is a look at one of the more important, and less understood, reports that you'll find during the summer months: the convective outlook.*

## Making sense of the AC

For the serious student of thunderstorms—and really, that should include all IFR pilots—the daily convective outlook (AC) is a must-read item for every briefing during the spring and summer. Filled out with pireps and real-time radar data, the AC is a first-rate source of informa-

**1** MKCSWODY 1 ALL OO ACUS 1 KMKC 021500

CONVECTIVE OUTLOOK...REF AFOS NMCGPH940

**2** VALID 021500 - 031200Z

**3** THERE IS A HIGH RISK OF SVR TSTMS BGNG THIS AFTERNOON AND CONTG INTO THE EVE OVR IL...IND...ERN MO...ERN IA...CNTRL AND SRN WI...LWR MI...WRN OH...AND WRN AND NRN KY. THE HIGH RISK IS TO THE RT OF A LN FM P02 JEF  CID LSE AWI APN MTC LUK FTK 20 S PAH P02

THERE IS A SLIGHT RISK OF SVR TSTMS TO THE RT OF A LN FM 20 N ROC JST CRW TUP 30 S MLU SAT 40 SSE DRT...CONT...40 S PO7 MAF FSM SZL FRM AXN INL

**4** GEN TSTMS ARE FCST TO THE RT OF A LN FM 90 S MRF INK FSI BVO GRI 60 N DVL...CONTD...80 N MWN LEB ABE WAL.

**5** OUTBREAK OF SVR TSTMS AND TORNADOES EXPCD FM ERN MO INTO THE GT LKS AREA AS A VERY STG UPR LVL **6** SYSTEM MOVES RPDLY EWD ACRS A VRY UNSTBL AMS WHERE SFC LI OF MINUS 7 TO MINUS 10 PROGD. **7** NEGLY TILTED MID/UPR LVL TROF NOW MOVG ACRS CNTRL PLAINS IS PROGD TO MOVE EWD 40 KT AS ASSOCD CDFNT SURGES EWD WHERE A PRONOUNCED SFC PRES RISE AND **8** FALL COUPLET IS ALREADY EVIDENT. FNT WILL ACT TO FOCUS SVR ACTVTY AS IT MOVS EWD INTO THE MID MS VLY WHILE THE SRN PTN OF THE BNDRY STALLS OVR TX. **9** LOW LVL MSTR ALREADY IN PLACE OVR HIGH RISK AREA WITH SFC DWPTS CURRENTLY RANGING FM MID 60S TO **10** LOW 70S. VRY STG MID LEVEL WND MAX OF 70 KT THRUSTING EWD ACRS KS INTO IL/IN BYE EVE EXPCD TO INCRS UPR LVL DVRGNC PAT FM IA INTO WI/MI/IL/IN. **11** STG MID LVL DRYING ALSO EVIDENT ACRS HIGH RISK AREA GIVING THREAT OF SVR TSTMS AND TORNADOES. DESTRUCTIVE TORNADOES ARE LIKELY WITH THESE TSTMS **12** SO STRONGLY WORDED PUBLIC AWARENESS STATEMENTS ARE IN ORDER TODAY TO EMPHASIZE THIS THREATENING SITUATION.

tion on conditions likely to spawn dangerous thunderstorms. Like its cousin, the area forecast, the AC is a broad-brush treatment but it has considerably more geographical detail. Moreover, the forecaster explains his thinking at length, making the AC a powerful tool for both avoiding thunderstorms and for learning about how and why they develop.

The AC is released three times a day by the National Severe Storms Forecast Center in Kansas City. It's available on DUAT both in text and graphic form. For the text, specify the Kansas City identifier (MKC) and request the AC. For the map, switch to the value-added mode and use the menu or specify D27. On DTC DUAT, the map is issued twice a day (1030Z) and 2100Z. Updates of actual conditions are issued as required and are available by requesting F300.

To show how to interpret this beast, we called up an AC and asked Larry Wilson, a senior forecaster at MKC's storm center with some 27 years of experience, to interpret it for us. Please refer to the reproduction of the report on the opposite page.

1. This line identifies the origin of the forecast as Kansas City. SWODY1 means severe weather outlook, day 1. The day 2—not as widely disseminated as the day 1, describes expected conditions for next day.

2. The day's first AC is issued at 0700Z with a valid time from 1200Z to 1200Z the following morning. Two updates follow, one at 1500Z and one at 1900Z. Amendments are issued as required. This forecast is the first update.

3. June 2 was one of the most active thunderstorm days of 1990. An upper level trough moving eastward across the plains into warm, moist air created an explosive environment for severe thunderstorms. Three-letter identifiers describe the area in which severe storms—surface gusts greater than 50 knots, hail 3/4 inch or larger, tornadoes—are likely. High risk days are relatively rare, especially over such a wide area.

4. An area of general thunderstorms covering a major portion of the central U.S. surrounded the high-risk area. This was definitely not a good day to be flying.

5. We use words like "outbreak" or "pronounced" or "particularly dangerous" to draw extraordinary attention to potentially severe conditions. An outbreak describes severe thunderstorms over an area of

two or more states where tornadoes are likely. Outbreak days are not common, occurring perhaps four or five times a year.

6. The lifted index is a good relative measure of atmospheric instability, with numbers between 0 and minus 4 representing thunderstorm potential. An LI of minus 7 to minus 10 is very unstable air.

7. When the lifted index is low and moist air is present, a "negatively tilted" upper air pattern is a red flag for impending storm development. A negative tilt occurs when the upper level jet stream changes direction sharply, thus accelerating lifting in an unstable airmass.

8. One effect of a negative tilt is to deepen a surface low pressure, causing a rapid pressure change (a couplet) as the system moves. The bigger the change, the higher the likelihood of strong storms. Surface stations reporting "pressure falling rapidly" often signal the onset of severe storms.

9. "Low level moisture already in place"—as evidenced by high dewpoints—is another warning signal. As the upper-level trough moves into the risk area, it brings cold air aloft over warm, moist air at the surface, increasing vertical development. On June 2, this explosive development occurred after 2000Z in Illinois.

10. "Very strong mid-level winds" are another bad sign. These so-called steering currents at the 500 millibar level push developing storms across favorable surface conditions, where they can intensify.

11. Mid-level drying creates the so-called dry line at the the surface. This further enhances vertical motion by causing significant contrast between two airmasses.

12. When we prepare the AC, we look for that rare combination of explosive conditions that can produce severe storms. This is the first time I'd ever advised strongly worded public statements to describe the threat. They turned out to warranted. On June 2, there were 200 reports of severe weather, including 68 tornadoes. Nine fatalities were reported in Illinois and Indiana.

Going over an AC in midsummer is a great way to learn more about thunderstorms. And hopefully, when it looks like this one, it'll be enough to convince you not to fly.

While we're on the subject of summertime phenomena, it bears noting that the NWS changed the format of some of its reports not too long ago.

In early 1993, the National Weather Service changed the format of in-flight weather advisories. These advisories are reported as Severe Weather Forecast Alerts (AWW), Convective Sigmets (WST), Sigmets (WS), Center Weather Advisories (CWA) or Airmets (WA). The information in these advisories is also included in the area forecast (FA), unless the advisory was issued after the FA was released or amended. Always compare the time of the advisory with the area forecast.

## Thunderstorm advisories

Severe weather forecast alerts (AWW) are usually combined with severe weather bulletins (WW) and define areas of possible severe thunderstorms or tornado activity. These advisories are unscheduled and are issued as required by the National Severe Storms Forecast Center in Kansas City.

Convective sigmets (WST) report thunderstorms and related conditions of tornadoes, heavy precipitation, hail and high surface winds. A WST is issued for:

• Tornadoes.
• Lines of thunderstorms.
• Embedded thunderstorms.
• Thunderstorm areas greater than or equal to thunderstorm intensity level 4 with an area of 40 percent or greater coverage.
• 3/4-inch or larger hail and/or wind gusts of 50 knots or greater.

Severe or greater turbulence, severe icing and low-level wind shear (gust fronts, downbursts, microbursts, etc.) are implied and aren't specified in the WST. Assume some or all of these elements will be present when a WST is issued.

Three convective sigmet bulletins are issued for the Eastern, Central and Western U.S. These bulletins are issued hourly at 55 minutes past the hour (H+55) and as special bulletins as needed. Each bulletin is valid for two hours or until superseded by the next hourly issuance.

Each hour, an outlook is made for each of the three convective sigmet regions. The outlook is a forecast and meteorological discussion for thunderstorm systems that are expected to require WST issuances two to six hours into the future. An outlook is always made for each of the three regions, even if it's a negative statement.

## Other hazardous conditions

Sigmets are issued for the following hazardous weather:

• Severe, extreme turbulence or clear air turbulence not associated with thunderstorms.

• Severe icing not associated with thunderstorms.

• Widespread dust storms, sandstorms or volcanic ash lowering surface and/or in-flight visibilities to less than three miles.

The center weather advisory (CWA) is an unscheduled in-flight, flow control, air traffic and air crew advisory. By the nature of its short lead time, the CWA isn't a flight planning product, but a forecast of conditions beginning within the next two hours. A CWA is issued:

• As a supplement to an existing sigmet, convective sigmet, airmet or area forecast.

• When an in-flight advisory has not been issued, but observed or expected conditions meet the criteria for a sigmet/airmet based on pilot reports and other sources.

• When observed or developing weather doesn't meet the criteria for a sigmet, convective sigmet or airmet, but pilot reports and other sources indicate the weather will adversely affect traffic flow in the Center's airspace.

An airmet is issued for any of the following conditions:
• Moderate icing.
• Moderate turbulence.
• Sustained winds of 30 knots or more at the surface.
• Widespread area of ceilings less than 1000 feet and/or visibility less than three miles.
• Extensive mountain obscurement.

However, if the above conditions are adequately forecast in the area forecast, an airmet won't be issued. Airmets are issued every six hours, with unscheduled amendments issued as needed. Each airmet has a fixed designator: Zulu for icing and freezing level data, Tango for turbulence, strong surface winds and wind shear, and Sierra for IFR conditions and mountain obscuration.

*Next we look at one of the more confusing products that the NWS puts out: another summertime special, the radar report. It's confusing not because the information is hard to understand, but because the streams of numbers and letters refer to locations on a map that the user probably can't see.*

## Decoding Radar Reports

Radar weather reports (RAREPs) are supposed to be a standard part of every preflight briefing. These reports are handy during prime thunderstorm season and can help you plan a campaign of thunderstorm avoidance.

The National Weather Service issues rareps (coded SD for Storm Detection) at 35 past each hour, with special reports issued as conditions warrant. The observations are from both NWS and ATC radar sites around the country. These observations are also used to generate the radar summary chart.

Rareps contain the following information on precipitation and thunderstorms: configuration, coverage, location, movement, and height of echoes; types and intensities of precipitation; and intensity trends. Since radar picks up precipitation only, information on cloud coverage, tops or bases isn't provided.

In a DUAT briefing, rareps appear in the Flight Hazards section. During a telephone briefing, the briefer should include all pertinent rareps (if not, ask). Not all radar sites issue rareps. For example, west of the Rockies, information is obtained from ATC radar, so only activity summaries (not rareps) are issued from these facilities.

## Rarep format

Let's review the format of a rarep, and then discuss some examples. All reports begin with the location identifier of the radar site and the UTC (Zulu) time of the observation.

Next is the echo pattern or configuration. These observations fall into three categories: cell, line and area.

• **Cell** - A single isolated area of precipitation that is clearly distinct from any surrounding echoes. Precipitation may or may not reach the ground.

• **Line** - An area of precipitation that is at least 30 miles long (either straight or curved), is at least five times as long as it is wide, with at least 30 percent coverage. Occasionally, observers report a fine line, which is a clear-air echo (usually free of precipitation and clouds), indicating a strong temperature/moisture boundary along a dry cold front.

• **Area** - A group of echoes all of which are similar in type, but not classified as a line. A spiral band area, for example, occurs near a hurricane.

• **Layer** - Similar to an area, but given a separate classification. This is a layer of stratiform precipitation that does not reach the ground.

## Precip coverage

Next on the report is the amount of precipitation coverage, which the observer estimates and reports in tenths. This is followed by type, intensity and intensity trend of the weather. The same weather symbols

# Selected SD coded data

**Echo pattern codes:**

| | |
|---|---|
| CELL | Single cell |
| LN | Line |
| FINE LN | Fine Line |
| AREA | Group of echoes |
| SPRL BAND | Spiral Band Area |
| LYR | Layer |

**Intensity Trend:**

- Decreasing    **NC** No Change
+ Increasing    **NEW** New echo

**Remarks:**

| | |
|---|---|
| LEWP | Line echo wave pattern |
| MA | Echoes mostly aloft |
| PA | Echoes partly aloft |
| MLT LVL | Melting level |
| WER | Weak echo region |
| BWER | Bounded weak echo pattern |

**Radar Status codes:**

| | |
|---|---|
| PPINE | Equipment normal - no echoes observed |
| PPINA | Observation not available |
| PPIOM | Out of service for maintenance |
| NE | No echoes observed |
| NA | Observation unavailable |
| NS | Non-significant echoes |
| RHINO | Range/height indicator inoperative |
| ROBEPS | Radar operation below standards |
| ARNO | Azimuth/range indicator inoperative |

**Radar Precipitation Intensity (VIP) Levels and rainfall (in/hr)**

| | Echo | Stratus | Convective |
|---|---|---|---|
| 1 | Weak | <0.1 | <0.2 |
| 2 | Moderate | 0.1-0.5 | 0.2-1.1 |
| 3 | Strong | 0.5-1.0 | 1.1-2.2 |
| 4 | Very Strong | 1.0-2.0 | 2.2-4.5 |
| 5 | Intense | 2.0-5.0 | 4.5-7.1 |
| 6 | Extreme | >5.0 | >7.1 |

used on the radar summary chart are also used here. The key is listed in *Aviation Weather Services*, AC 00-45C.

The type of precipitation is recorded first, e.g., TRW is thunderstorm, followed by the intensity, e.g., + for heavy. The trend symbols, (+ for increasing, - for decreasing, etc.) follow and are separated from the intensity by a slash mark. Precipitation intensities are also listed and are assigned a number from 1 to 6, with 1 as weak and 6 as extreme. This appears in digitized form at the end of the report.

The location of convective activity from the station is given in relation to true north and in nautical miles from the station. The diameter or width of the echo pattern (in nautical miles) follows when azimuth and range define only the centerline of the pattern. For example, 20W is a line with a total width of 20 nm; whereas D20 is a convective echo 20 nm in diameter.

The direction and speed of movement of the echoes is next. This observation may also show movement of individual cells (C) and/or movement of an area (A). Movement of a line or area indicates the overall movement of the activity; movement of a single cell is within that line or area.

Following this are the maximum tops (in feet msl) and distance in degrees and nautical miles from the station. Uniform tops within a stable air mass are reported as U. Top information is for precipitation, not the clouds themselves. In a building thunderstorm, the cloud and precipitation tops are usually close together. However, in a dissipating thunderstorm, the precipitation tops can be thousands of feet below the cloud tops.

Pertinent remarks on the weather are next. These remarks can include observations about hail, strong winds, tornado activity and other adverse weather associated with the echoes. For instance, a hook-shaped echo may be associated with a tornado and gusty winds may indicate a line echo bulge, which means a portion of the squall line has moved out ahead of the rest.

Also noted in the remarks are instances when precipitation isn't reaching the ground, and the remark indicates whether the precipitation is aloft or mostly aloft. The bases of the precipitation are in hundreds of feet msl.

## Precip intensity

The precipitation intensity appears last in the report. This is coupled with one or more letters on the line following the rarep, which refer to a grid square on the overlay chart described below. Although meteorologists use this digitized information to prepare radar summary charts, you can use it to draw a picture of precipitation intensity and location.

You can do this by keying the digits to a specialized grid overlay chart centered on the reporting station and oriented to true north. Each 22-nm-square box on the grid is identified by two letters, with the first representing the row of the box and the second letter representing the column. Box MM (row 13 of 26, column 13 of 26) is centered over the reporting station.

The intensity level appears after these letters. Each block on the grid is assigned an intensity level from 1 to 6. Level 1 is assigned when 20 percent of a box contains precipitation. Levels 8 and 9 are used for echoes of unknown intensity beyond the 125-nm range of the radar.

For example, MO1 means the box located in row M and column O (same row, two columns over: 44 miles due east of the station) with precipitation at the maximum level of 1. A code with several numbers, such as KJ2234, indicates precipitation in four consecutive boxes in the same row (left to right): KJ (Level 2), KK (Level 2), KL (Level 3) and KM (Level 4).

Plotting this information helps visualize the location and intensity of severe weather. But even if you don't have access to such a grid overlay, you can use the codes to get a mental picture of precipitation intensity. For example, an area of Levels 5 or 6, with 100 percent coverage (a solid line with extreme conditions) should be avoided.

Let's decode some examples:

**OKC 1525 CELL RW-/NEW 165/80 D8 C0000 MT 160 ^QO1=**
Radar report for Oklahoma City, OK at 1525 UTC. A cell of light rain showers, newly developed at 165 degrees, 80 nm, is eight miles in diameter. The cell movement is from 0 degrees at 0 knots (stationary). The maximum tops of the precipitation are 16,000 feet, with a Level 1 echo in box QO.

**ICT 1526 AREA 4TRW+/- 93/150 100/90 25W C2320 MT 230 AT 98/ 100**
**AREA 2TRW/NEW 352/165 15/120 25W C0000 MT 250 AT 9/120 MOSTLY TRWU ^FK99 GM9 LR29 MQ229 NQ1=**
Radar report for Wichita, KS at 1526 UTC. An area of echoes; four-tenths coverage of thunderstorms and heavy rain showers, decreasing at 93 degrees, 150 nm and 100 degrees, 90 nm; 25 miles wide. Cell movement from 230 degrees at 20 knots. The maximum tops are 23,000 feet at 98 degrees, 100 nm from the station.

Also, another area with two-tenths coverage of thunderstorms and rain showers, newly developed at 352 degrees, 165 nm and 15 degrees, 120 nm; 25 miles wide. Cell movement from 0 degrees at 0 knots. The maximum tops are 25,000 feet at 9 degrees, 120 nm from the station. Remarks note that the precipitation is mostly thunderstorms and unknown intensity rain showers (denoted by the 9s).

### SEP 1528 CELL TRWX/+ 192/69 D25 C2808 MT 330
### AREA 1RW/NEW 77/75 214/70 105W C2510 MT 200 AT 335/31 ^LL2 ML2 OL10002 PK253 QL4=

Stephenville, TX radar report at 1528 UTC. A cell of echoes of thunderstorms and intense rain showers, increasing at 192 degrees, 69 nm; 25 miles in diameter. Cell movement from 280 degrees at 8 knots. The maximum tops are 33,000 feet.

Also, an area of echoes, one-tenth coverage of rain showers, newly developed at 77 degrees, 75 nm and 214 degrees, 70 nm; 105 miles wide. Cell movement from 250 degrees at 10 knots. The maximum tops are 20,000 feet at 335 degrees, 31 nm from the station.

### TIK SD NO CURRENT DATA

The current radar report for Tinker AFB in Oklahoma City, OK is not available.

### AMA 1531 PPINE=

Amarillo, TX radar report at 1531 UTC, no echoes were observed.

Use rareps with the radar summary chart to determine the severity and location of convective activity. Areas of what appear to be solid echoes on the chart may actually contain holes. For example, an area that shows a solid line of moderate precipitation may in fact contain, according to the rarep, widely scattered light precipitation. While the radar summary chart plots general areas and movement of precipitation, a rarep provides more precise information.

Keep in mind that rareps are observations, not forecasts. Convective activity moves fast, so contact a facility with real-time weather radar for updates when airborne.

*The last topic we'll cover in this chapter concerns those problematic footnotes to aviation, Notices to Airmen. These can range from the annoying to the truly bizarre. (Remember when the government decided not to allow the body of the late Phillipine ruler Ferdinand Marcos to be returned to the Phillipines? There was actually a notam concerning it at the time.)*

*Even though they sometimes seem more trouble than they're worth, it pays to check the notam file whenever you fly. Failure to do so will catch up with you, sooner or later.*

## All About Notams

Unless you happen to like excruciating detail, it's hard to get very excited about notams. And why should you? Ninety-nine times out of 100, notams contain information that, while nice to know, is not nearly as interesting as what the weather is doing. Except...that one time in a hundred when not knowing about an airport closure, a navaid outage or a frequency revision might ruin your whole day.

The records are peppered with accidents in which people have been killed and aircraft destroyed because the pilot overlooked some critical safety-of-flight detail buried in the notams.

Most pilots grudgingly admit that notams are important, even if they are boring. Unfortunately, milking the notam system of its information is time-consuming and confusing. Adding to the difficulty is the fact that there are three categories of notams, each requiring you to jump through specific hoops. If you don't know what to look for and where, you might miss big chunks of the pie and that in turn could cause you to miss big chunks of your airplane.

## Alphabet soup

As with so many other things the government gets its hands on, notams are organized (not necessarily logically) by alphabetical designators. The most basic distinction made between notams is that there are two classes, some available only via the FAA's computer system and others published and routinely updated through the mail.

Notams not yet published but available electronically through the computer FSS specialists use (known as"Service A") are called Class I notams; Class II notams are published in a book called—what else?—Notices to Airmen. Some notams eventually find their way into the A/FD, too. The notams book is available by subscription from the Government Printing Office for $79 per year and it's issued every 15 days. Call the GPO at 202-783-3238 and have your Visa or MasterCard ready.

It's critical for the IFR pilot to understand that the FSS briefer will give you only Class I notams, the ones that automatically appear on his or her screen. If you want additional notams, you'll have to ask. And you'll have to know what to ask for. But more on that later.

The next stop on our alphabet soup adventure is "distant" (D) and "local" (L) notams. This pertains to how widely notam information is disseminated. Notam D information is placed on the FAA's computer system and is available to all Flight Service Stations. However, notam L information is only available if an FSS is within a 200-nautical-mile radius of the airfield issuing the notam. But how can you tell whether your destination airfield has notam D or L service?

The only way is to look in the Airport/Facility Directory to see if there's a section symbol (§) in front of the airport name. If the section symbol is shown, the airport has notam D service. If not, only notam Ls will be issued.

The new AFSSs don't subscribe to the 200-mile limitation for notam Ls. A so-called "family" of AFSSs will share the notam L information. There are two ways to find out if the AFSS will have notam Ls. The first is to ask the briefer and the second is to check the A/FD for the destination airport. The notam file information is contained in the communications section.

One important point to remember is that the D and L designation sometimes has more to do with the notam service available at the airport (D versus L) than with the gravity of the information contained in the notam.

Let's take an extreme example. Your destination is a mythical Three-Mile-Island Airport. The Airport/Facility Directory shows no section symbol, so notam D service isn't available. There's an FSS at your home drome, 300 miles from TMI. You get a thorough briefing before you depart, including checking for notams. The briefer tells you there are none. But, as luck would have it, there's been a radiation leak at the FBO, and the airport manager has issued a notam closing the field.

Here's the kicker. Since TMI doesn't have notam D service, your local FSS won't have access to the airport manager's notam; TMI is outside the 200-mile radius required for notam Ls. The briefer just won't have the information available to him, and there's no way for him to get to it unless he calls another FSS within 200 miles of TMI. That's not likely to happen unless you ask nicely and the briefer is in an especially good mood. Granted, that's an extreme example. But it does show the holes in the system.

## Forgotten but not gone

Perhaps the most neglected notams are those issued by the FAA's Flight Data Center (FDC). These notams describe changes to instrument charts and procedures, both en route and terminal. It's nice to know when an airway's been rerouted or when a missed approach procedure's been changed. Or how about when an MDA or DH has been raised by a few hundred feet?

FDC notams also describe special notices such as procedures for flying into Oshkosh or temporary flight restrictions for the Boston Marathon. These notams are issued every 15 days and actually make pretty interesting reading.

Since the FDC notams are published, they're Class II notams; Flight Service won't give them to you unless you make a special request and even then, you might not get what you want.

Case in point: The Lakeland VORTAC was out of service. An FDC notam was published changing the missed approach procedure for the ILS RWY 5. The existing miss took you to an intersection defined by the VORTAC. The new procedure called for a turn direct to the LOM for the published hold.

We decided to "press to test" and called the St. Petersburg FSS to ask for FDC notams at Lakeland. Guess what? We were told that there weren't any. Since we knew this was incorrect, we asked the briefer if he was using the published book of notams or he if was just looking at the FDC notams on the computer screen. He replied that the ones on the screen would be all we'd need.

We asked to talk to a supervisor. After 15 minutes of pleading, we finally got the notam. Here's the point: If the FAA prints the notam, you're expected to subscribe to it. Even though the FSS specialist is required to give you that information if you request it, that's not the way the system actually works. That little book of notams may be rat-holed far from the briefer's screen and he may not be thrilled about getting up to hunt for it. But remember, the pilot, not the briefer, is responsible for obtaining "all available information."

To pilots who use Jeppesen plates, the 15-day publication cycle of FDC notams should sound familiar. Jepp revisions are timed to coincide with FDC notams so any new information should appear right on the plate. This makes things a bit easier, as long as you don't mind posting all those changes. Of course, you'll still have to consult Jepp's FDC notam sheets for any special notices.

We noted above that FSS won't give you FDC notams unless you ask. However, we should add that FDC notams issued after the deadline for the current book will appear on the briefer's screen. The briefer will have FDC notams for airports within a 400-mile radius of the FSS. If your destination is farther than that from the FSS giving you the briefing, you might have to make a special request.

One of the favorite tricks CFIIs have is to hand a student a current set of NOS charts, as well as the change notice that's in effect at the time. Then I ask a very simple question: what's the MDA for the NDB RWY 25 approach into Patrick Henry Airport? More often than not the student will check the table of contents in the change notice. So far so good. Checking the table is the only way to tell whether the approach has been eliminated. Finding nothing in the changes, the student moves to the approach plate and announces that the MDA is 500 feet. Not good. The FDC notam gives a new MDA of 600 feet. That's certainly nice to know.

## Loran notams

In these days of cheap area navigation, more and more pilots are relying heavily on their lorans for real-world primary navigation. Knowing that the signal is being broadcast correctly can be critical.

There is a way to check the status of those loran chains. The Coast Guard reports loran problems to the U.S. Notam Office. These notams are then placed in the FAA's computer under the location identifier LRN.

Unfortunately, these notams are only given if the pilot requests them, and many FSS specialists aren't familiar with them. If the specialist briefing you hasn't accessed them before, you may have to walk him or her through the procedure. Just give the briefer the computer code that's used to access the information: RQ LRN NTM. One word of warning: This trick won't work with DUAT. You'll just get a message saying LRN isn't a real place.

There's one small catch with these notams. The loran chains are identified by number. Check FAA Advisory Circular 20-121 or the AIM, paragraph 20, to translate these numbers into more useful terms. The AIM will also give you a telephone number for each loran chain. This number will connect you to a recorded briefing that will describe any problems the chain might be experiencing.

For example, even though the northeast U.S. chain (9960) had no current notams, a call to their answering machine warned of lock-on and tracking problems caused by sunspots and a powerful Navy transmitter in the North Atlantic. The entire message lasted about two minutes.

## Phone ahead

If you're going to get the maximum information through the notam system and elsewhere, you'll have to do a bit of homework. Prior to calling FSS or logging onto DUAT, check the current A/FD to see if your destination has notam D service. If it doesn't, you may have to do some digging. Make sure you've got current plates and charts and that you've reviewed the appropriate FDC notams and special notices. Remember, if your destination is farther than 400 miles from the FSS, you may have to make a special request for FDC notams at your destination.

Even a phone call to your local FSS may not be enough to get all the information that you'll need for your flight, especially if you're venturing far from home. Here's a technique that may make a difference. Call the airport manager, the chief pilot or a CFI at your destination. They'll have the most current information. It may not be "official," but it's a good idea to plan on the bad stuff, and believe the good stuff once you see it. You can get the appropriate phone numbers from several sources including *Flight Guide, Jepp Guide* and the *AOPA Aviation USA*. Finally, when inbound, give a call to the Unicom or tower to find out if anything has changed since you took off.

It may take a good deal of digging to find all of that elusive "pertinent information," but it's usually worth it. The information's out there. It's up to the pilot to find it.

# • Section Two •

# Survival
# Strategies

# Making the
# Tough Choices

E*very time an instrument pilot launches (or even plans to launch) into bad weather, he or she is taking on a series of potential life-or-death deci-sions. Is the weather more than I or my airplane can handle? Can I really make it to the destination safely? The weather just got worse...should I turn around or keep going?*

*Any instrument pilot knows that the actual skills involved in flying IFR are fairly simple, though demanding if the job is to be done right. The tough part is developing a finely tuned sense of judgment.*

*Knowing when to call it quits may well be the single most important skill an instrument pilot can have.*

*All too often, though, pilots will defer, delay, and otherwise try to get out of making those tough choices. Sometimes, failure to face up to the facts can prove fatal.*

*In this chapter, we'll look at decision making, the go/no go decision, and personal limits.*

## Hope Springs Eternal

Pilots are a hopeful lot. We hope that the engine will keep running; we hope that we won't run out of gas; and we hope that a briefer's weather forecast of lousy weather was just a manifestation of his conservative nature ... especially when we have to get somewhere in a hurry.

During the summer, when the combination of moisture and heat generate thunderstorms in most parts of the country, we also hope that somehow we'll be able to get through or around those nasty atmospheric disturbances.

When you study the transcripts of thunderstorm-related accidents, you can almost hear the hope in pilots' voices as they talk to air traffic controllers about conditions up ahead, seemingly unaware that the controller can't really tell them much. The examples that follow are from actual accident reports. The communications have been edited for clarity, but the essence of each situation remains.

## New England bound

A Piper Comanche departed its home base in Florida with four on board, bound for an autumn vacation in New England. The preflight briefing included information about an area of rain showers and scattered thunderstorms along the route of flight.

After a fuel stop in Norfolk, Virginia, N54P continued northeastward and the pilot was soon talking to New York Center. (Possible pilot thoughts are in parentheses).

*N54P:* New York, Five-Four-Papa with a request.

*Center:* Go ahead, Five-Four-Papa.

*N54P:* If it works, I'd like direct Atlantic City and then Victor 229 JFK. You showing any weather from our present position to Atlantic City? (I hope there isn't any, and if there is, I hope he can steer us away from the worst of it.)

*Center:* I'm not showing any weather from your present position that far north.

*N54P:* Okay, ah, we're in moderate showers at this time. (If there's nothing on radar, I'm not going to worry about it.)

Two minutes later, the controller noticed that N54P's altitude had changed and brought it to the pilot's attention.

*Center:* Ah, Five-Four-Papa, the Atlantic City altimeter is two niner seven two. Your altitude readout indicates six thousand six hundred.

*N54P:* Okay, we got into some descending air. We're coming back now and two nine seven two, thank you.

The descending air apparently continued. The Comanche was handed off to another sector, and when the pilot checked in, he mentioned the altitude discrepancy.

*N54P:* Ah, New York, Comanche Five-Four-Papa, we're at six thousand six hundred, trying to get back to seven thousand. We're in some pretty heavy turbulence at this time.

*Center:* Five-Four-Papa, I missed your comment, say again.

*N54P:* We're in some heavy turbulence now. (I'm glad there was nothing on his radar. I hope we'll be out of this soon.)

No more was heard from Five-Four-Papa. The airplane was upset, the pilot lost control and the Comanche came apart before it hit the ground.

## Houston approach

Then there's N500CC, an A-36 Bonanza, bound from Dallas to Houston one April morning. The pilot checked the weather the night before, and was informed of a cold front forecast to pass through the area about the time he'd be in the air, with the usual mention of showers and thunderstorms. No further weather information was obtained before takeoff. We join the communications as the Bonanza checks in with Houston Approach Control.

*N500CC:* Houston Approach, Five-Hundred-Charlie-Charlie with you at four thousand.

*Approach:* Five-Hundred-Charlie-Charlie, expect vectors for the NDB one six approach at Andrau, Hobby altimeter two niner eight six.

*N500CC:* Two niner eight six, and how do we look on our present heading for getting through this stuff? (I hope he's right. I'm sure getting bounced around up here.)

*Approach:* I'm not depicting any weather on my scope, Five-Hundred-Charlie-Charlie.

In the next three minutes, there was considerable conversation between the controller and two other flights heading for the same airport. A strong cell lay just to the north of the airport and other flights were diverting to Houston-Hobby International Airport. Despite what the pilot of N500CC must have overheard, the following conversation took place:

*N500CC:* Approach, Five-Hundred-Charlie-Charlie, can we take a cut toward Andrau now and stay out of trouble?

*Approach:* Five-Hundred-Charlie-Charlie, roger, deviate at your discretion, maintain four thousand.

*N500CC:* Approach, if we take up a heading of one five zero, will it be okay? (I hope so, because I've got to get on the ground in a hurry.)

*Approach:* Ah, one five zero, ah, at your discretion Five-Hundred-Charlie-Charlie. I can't tell on my radar.

After another three minutes, N500CC called again:

*N500CC:* Approach, Bonanza Five-Hundred-Charlie-Charlie, I show twenty-one north of Andrau. We're in real heavy rain, pretty good chop.

*Approach:* Five-Hundred-Charlie-Charlie, say again, you were cut out.

*N500CC:* Yes sir, we're twenty north of Andrau, ah, getting some lightning, some real good chop, some very heavy rain.

*Approach:* Charlie-Charlie, roger, what are your intentions? Do you want to continue on to Andrau?

*N500CC:* Well, I would like to get into Andrau and get out of this stuff (I hope, I hope). Ah, you're not showing some pretty good cells?

*Approach:* Well, my whole area is covered with cells. I'm not differentiating between them.

*N4CE:* Approach, this Four-Charlie-Echo, we're on the procedure turn outbound. It's pretty smooth, heavy rain and a little bit of hail, that's all [that's all?!]. Some lightning, but it's pretty smooth.

*N500CC:* Okay sir, we heard that, ah, this is Five-Hundred-Charlie-Charlie, we'll continue inbound to Andrau.

*Approach:* Five-Hundred-Charlie-Charlie, maintain three thousand. You're number two on the approach, expect to hold north of Andrau on the final approach course at three thousand. It'll be right turns, one minute legs. Time now is 1506, expect approach clearance at ah, 1520.

*N500CC:* Zero-Charlie-Charlie. (Damn, what a time to get a hold! ... I hope it won't take very long to get those other flights on the ground.)

It didn't take long, but the other flights didn't get on the ground either. Less than five minutes passed and approach control advised N500CC that the airplane ahead of him executed a missed approach due to weather. He asked Charlie-Charlie what his intentions were.

*N500CC:* Send us over to Hobby sir.

*Approach:* Five-Hundred-Charlie-Charlie, fly present heading and maintain three thousand, vector for the ILS Runway 13 Right at Hobby.

*N500CC:* Roger, and we're running into some pretty heavy stuff. (I sure hope he can see it on radar. This is getting rough.)

*Approach:* Five-Hundred-Charlie-Charlie, the aircraft about six miles in front of you reported a severe updraft about four miles north of your present position.

*N500CC:* You ain't kidding ... can you get me out of this?! (I hope you can. This is more than I bargained for!)

*Approach:* Turn right, Charlie-Charlie, heading two seven zero.

*N500CC:* Damn!

Very shortly thereafter, N500CC hit the ground at very high speed.

## Mississippi delta

One more example. This pilot, flying Bonanza N46D, planned an IFR flight from northern Florida to Vicksburg, Mississippi one day in May. Here's a portion of his preflight briefing:

*Briefer:* All right sir, looks like a convective sigmet is in effect for your route of flight. There's some very solid activity over around Pensacola and the Alabama area is really solid. That area is drifting to the east and could be some problems for you.

*N46D:* Have you had anybody going through, getting vectors around it or anything? (I hope there's some way to get through. I have to be in Vicksburg on time.)

*Briefer:* Well, I haven't talked to anybody up there that came down this way at all this morning, but the radar and the current conditions would indicate that there is going to be some activity through there, quite heavy locally. I understand that the forecast is going to be amended before long to show those thunderstorms building.

*N46D:* It's going to get worse?

*Briefer:* Yeah, it looks kind of bad up there for the next two or three hours, yes sir.

*N46D:* Okay, I'll call back to file.

When the pilot called back an hour and a half later to file, the briefer apparently remembered his previous conversation. After recording the flight plan information, he reminded the pilot of the weather on his route: "All right sir, and those thunderstorms up there have developed tops to around forty-six thousand now."

The pilot acknowledged that rather scary fact, then decided to press on. We pick up the conversation as N46D is approaching the Pensacola area. He's just checking in with a new controller.

*N46D:* Center, Bonanza Four-Six-Delta with you at eight thousand.

*Approach:* Four-Six-Delta, this is Pensacola Approach, ident. The altimeter is two niner eight niner.

*N46D:* Two niner eight niner, and are you painting any weather off to my right here, ahead about ten or fifteen miles? (I can see some dark clouds over there. Probably one of those big storms. I hope he can see it on radar.)

*Approach:* Ah, Four-Six-Delta, in the way of weather, ah, no. I don't have very much at all on the scope up that way. Well, maybe about ten or fifteen miles off to your right but nothing else.

*N46D:* Okay, thank you. Looks kinda boogery up there, but not bad where I am right now. (I hope he'll let me know if anything bad shows up. I'm on the gauges now and I hope he won't let me run into a thunderstorm.)

Another handoff, this time to Houston Center, and the pilot of N46D reminded the new controller that he couldn't see where he was going.

*N46D:* Center, Bonanza Four-Six-Delta with you at eight thousand, we're on the gauges. (I hope this controller will be able to see the thunderstorms on his radar.)

*Center:* Roger, Four-Six-Delta, Mobile altimeter is two niner eight five.

*N46D:* Roger, two niner eight five. (I hope he heard me say that I'm on the gauges. Better tell him again).

*N46D:* Ah, Center, Four-Six-Delta's on the gauges, okay?

*Center:* Four-Six-Delta, roger.

It appears that the pilot of N46D became even more concerned about where he was in relation to the weather which he characterized earlier as "kinda boogery," and just as concerned about the controller keeping him away from the bad stuff.

Thirteen minutes later, he transmitted once again that he was going on the gauges (and apparently still hoping that the controller would keep him clear of the severe weather). Five minutes after that, Center requested a transponder code change, but N46D didn't respond ... the airplane was on the ground, totally destroyed.

## Hopeful expectations

The previous examples were chosen from a group of similar cases, all of them clearly exhibiting pilot hopes or expectations that air traffic control radar would vector them clear of severe weather. In almost every case, the pilots placed themselves in the uncomfortable situation of flying in clouds which contained thunderstorms—and here's the important part—in airplanes with no storm-detection equipment on board.

In almost every case, these pilots were briefed on the presence or potential of convective activity along their routes of flight. When the thunderstorm materialized, the pilots appeared to hope that ATC radar would save the day.

There's a cold, hard fact of today's IFR operations that all pilots must understand and keep firmly in mind when flying through thunderstorm-infested areas: ATC radar is intended for one major task—the separation of airplanes, nothing else.

Time was when a good radar controller could actually pick out the soft spots in areas of precipitation displayed on the scope, but that was in the days when radar was not computerized.

Pilots must understand that controllers see only computer-generated returns these days. When areas of precipitation are displayed, they are quantified at only two preset levels (grossly oversimplified for our purposes): some precipitation—which can mean anything from light drizzle to heavy rain—and a possible thunderstorm.

These displays show up on the controller's screen as areas of radial lines (precipitation), with, occasionally, some capital Hs embedded in them. The radial lines indicate the general dimensions of an area in which some precipitation is occurring, while the Hs represent the computer's recognition of higher rainfall intensity, which might be a thunderstorm.

Pilots using onboard storm detection equipment might be able to interpret what they see and fly safely through precip areas or navigate clear of them.

## What are your expectations?

There are two questions to be considered: first, can you depend on a controller to keep you out of convective trouble? (The answer is a resounding NO!) Second, can you expect to get safely through an area of precipitation pointed out by a controller? (The answer can only be maybe. It depends on how nasty the weather really is; how good you are at flying in heavy turbulence; how strong your airplane is and how much discomfort you and your passengers can tolerate.)

Given the high probability that a pilot's insistence on penetrating a known area of convective activity is an investigative operation (a flight into the unknown), it seems good sense to leave that kind of test flying to those who get paid for it.

This is a matter of understanding and respecting the limitations of one of the systems we use every time we fly IFR. There's only one way to absolutely avoid the kind of unhappiness experienced by the three pilots in our examples and that is to never let yourself get painted into a corner. Don't fly in an area of thunderstorm activity when you can't see what's ahead of you. If you don't have the unique vision provided by onboard equipment, don't place your safety dependence on someone (e.g., a controller) who can't do much more than let you know there's something out there.

## Consider the options

The options are: (1) climb above the obscuring cloud layer and circumnavigate the storms visually, (2) get below the clouds so that you can see the rain shafts, or (3) wait until conditions improve. Considering the limited altitude capability of most light airplanes, and the dangers inherent in trying to fly beneath conditions like this, option #3 has a lot going for it. There are indeed many times when he who looks and flies away, lives to fly another day.

## Asking tough questions

An instrument pilot must never lose sight of the fact that he or she is, alone, responsible for the flight. The only one who is going to keep you safe is *you*.

Many instrument pilots admit they feel a great deal of uncertainty when making weather decisions. This isn't surprising when you consider it's possible to fail all of the weather questions on the FAA written exam and still pass. Is this a good procedure? We don't think so.

It's also possible to get an instrument rating without ever having flown in the clouds, yet you're authorized to go out and fly any approach to minimums the day you get the rating. Before recommend-ing anyone for the instrument flight test, a good instructor should make every effort to seek out and fly in weather with them.

Pilots ask what they can do to improve weather decision-making and still use their aircraft for efficient transportation. No matter how much you learn about meteorology and its effect on air operations, and no matter how much experience you have, the secret to longevity depends on your answers to the following questions every time you fly IFR:

• If the forecast goes bust and conditions are worse than expected, what are my options? Do I have a viable out? Do I have the capability and does the airplane have the endurance to alter my flight toreach better conditions?

• Am I willing to fly single-engine IFR if I know that 200-300 foot ceilings are along my planned route? Am I willing to accept a dead-stick glide in the event of engine failure and take my chances on what lies below the overcast in reduced visibility, especially at night?

These questions emphasize that you must be prepared for adverse situations and be ready to make the decisions that ensure safe flight. Nobody else can make the go/no-go decision. That alone is your judgment.

*We all know about planning for alternates and when it's required. Even though it has no real meaning to ATC (see the first volume in the series,* Sweet Talking the System*), the alternate is something to always keep in mind when planning an IFR flight.*

*But there's really more than one kind of alternate: we're not talking about a different destination, but a whole alternate course of action, one that leaves you a way out of a bad situation.*

*In this section contributing editor and CFII John Conrad passes on some thoughts on the fine art of leaving yourself an escape route in case of trouble.*

## Planning for the *Real* Alternate

During the last twelve IFR cross countries I've flown during refresher training, not one pilot has prepared an alternate flight plan.

The alternate flight plan I'm talking about has nothing to do with the alternate airport filed on the FAA flight plan, which notifies ATC of your intentions in case you miss the approach at your destination and have a communications failure.

An alternate flight plan is your escape route in case a problem or emergency forces you to divert from your intended destination. If you always have an alternative flight plan, you're one of a few pilots that do.

Under normal circumstances, if you miss the approach, you tell ATC your second choice for an airport. But if you cannot communicate, you must go to your filed alternate. Therefore, it's important that the alternate listed on your flight plan is where you really want to go with a radio failure.

Assuming you have enough fuel, an airport 150 miles away that has VFR weather and two 10,000 foot runways is better than one with a steep NDB approach near your original destination.

## Refresher scenario

Before every IFR cross country, I give the pilot a complete weather briefing and then we depart. As the flight progresses, I introduce problems. Icing is usually encountered first. If carburetor heat is available and the pilot doesn't use it, I reduce the throttle to simulate the effects of carb ice.

Next, I cover the airspeed indicator to simulate its failure if pitot heat isn't used. If the pilot doesn't get us out of the icing, I turn off the communications radios and tell him that ice broke off the antenna. The navigation antennas are next to go.

I continue reducing engine power to simulate the accumulation of ice until the airplane descends to the lowest safe altitude, at which point I have the pilot take the hood off. This exercise is not designed to scare or humiliate anyone, but to determine if he/she has made an alternate plan for these emergencies and can execute the plan under stress.

I've seen some clever examples of quick thinking, like the fellow who used the Flite-phone to call ATC after the communications radios quit. Unfortunately, he continued to fly into deteriorating conditions.

## Plan to escape

The purpose of this training is to get pilots to run from trouble, instead of pressing further into it. If you fly long enough, there will come a time when you need an escape route.

This philosophy is discussed in Robert N. Buck's book, *Weather Flying*, where he recommends that a beginning instrument pilot fly only actual IFR departures to VFR conditions on top.

After the pilot is comfortable with this, he/she can fly when both the departure airport and the destination are IFR, but when the route is VFR. The pilot progresses to IFR-on-top and finally to IMC en route.

During the early stages of an instrument pilot's career, there should always be a way out so that he/she can climb, descend or land short of the destination and sort things out in VFR conditions.

Buck's philosophy should be part of every instrument flight. Regardless of where you depart or where you plan to land, there is always some place where the weather is better than on your route, and some places where it's worse. Not only do you need to know the weather en route, but where there is better weather and suitable terrain in case of an emergency. The conventional weather briefing does not ordinarily provide this.

## Briefing falls short

The briefing begins with sigmets and airmets about icing, thunderstorms and turbulence. If you're looking for an excuse to cancel the flight, you'll have one right here. When there's enough ice in the atmosphere to chill a martini and when there's enough turbulence to shake it, a sigmet is issued.

The possibility of icing, turbulence or thunderstorms doesn't mean you should automatically cancel a flight. The location and movement of thunderstorms can be plotted on the radar summary chart. Turbulence is uncomfortable, but seldom life threatening. Pilot reports verify its existence and, like thunderstorms, areas of turbulence can be avoided.

Icing, however, can sneak up on you with disastrous results. An MEA higher than the freezing level can be safe provided there is an escape route to lower terrain or warmer conditions.

The standard FAA weather briefing tells what could happen in the worst case scenario, but it tells very little about what the weather actually is. Unless you routinely ask for pireps, you'll never know the actual conditions along the airway. You need to know the weather for the stations underneath your route and most importantly, you need to know those areas within the range of your airplane with better weather.

Once you have a thorough grasp of the weather, do your preliminary flight planning on a VFR chart. Find an area where the most favorable weather and the most favorable terrain coincide. Ask yourself, "If I have to divert, where am I going and how am I going to get there?" Answering this question makes you calculate the most important flight plan of the trip: the one that doesn't take you to your destination.

## Know when to retreat

On a recent IFR refresher cross country, the pilot of a Beech Bonanza was flying from Los Angeles to Sacramento, California. The fictitious weather called for severe conditions inland.

The pilot struggled up the airways with ice hanging off the airplane and equipment failures galore. With no communications radios, and no idea of the actual weather at Sacramento, he attempted an NDB approach and lost control during the procedure turn.

In frustration, he took the hood off and shouted, "Well, what would *you* have done?" As he calmed himself, I told him I would have climbed to 6500 feet and turned to 210.

"Then what would you have done?" he demanded.

"Nothing," I replied. I pointed to the weather he had copied from the briefing. Monterey and the entire northwest coast of California was VFR.

Sometimes the most profound victory comes from a well planned and organized retreat.

*In the first section we took a look at weather briefings. Let's visit that subject again, and see how best to make use of the information a briefer gives you to make a valid, informed and intelligent go/no go decision.*

*Corporate pilot Brian Jacobson here passes on his personal methods for decision-making using weather briefing information.*

## Decision-making and the weather

I once flew with a corporate pilot who's attitude was, "It doesn't matter what the weather is doing, we have to go anyhow." This man's perspective was wrong on all accounts, but I strongly suspected weather interpretation wasn't one of his finer skills. Whenever I flew with him I examined the weather carefully, because I knew he did little more than ask for the sequences and terminal forecasts at the beginning of the day. If we made an en route stop, he rarely checked weather. Attitudes like that eventually get pilots into trouble.

When it comes to planning an IFR flight too little knowledge can be very dangerous. There are so many things that can go wrong in a short period that you must be sure of what you're doing, what you expect the weather will do and what you plan to do if the weather doesn't cooperate. The best way to accomplish this is to make the most of a weather briefing. Get all the information you need to make informed decisions.

The FAA tries to ensure the quality of weather briefings from flight service stations is the same throughout the country by using three types of briefings: standard, abbreviated and outlook. Theoretically, one of these briefings will serve your needs, but I've found a good briefing depends on several things, including the skill and experience of the flight service specialist.

## Press for what you need

When planning an IFR flight, know exactly what information you need and press the briefer if he/she doesn't give it to you. When the weather is IFR, briefers are usually busy and in a hurry to get to many waiting calls. They might try to summarize the situation.

For example, a briefer might tell you thunderstorms are forecast along your route. Some briefers think the T word is enough reason for everyone to stay on the ground. But if you pump the briefer for more information you might find that while the forecasts call for a chance of thunderstorms at your destination, none are showing up on radar, nor is any terminal reporting any. Would I cancel a flight based on a simple summary like that? No, I would need much more information.

According to the *Airman's Information Manual*, flight service station briefers may translate and interpret available forecasts and reports directly into terms describing the weather conditions which you can expect along your flight route and at your destination. The problem is you can get different interpretations from different specialists, much like you can watch two different meteorologists on television and get two different pictures.

That's why it's important to know about weather and make your own decisions. If you let a briefer make decisions for you, you won't fly IFR very often.

## Briefing sources

I use The Weather Channel (TWC) and DUAT for most of my briefings. The night before a flight, TWC gives me the location of systems and fronts and what to expect the next day. DUAT provides forecasts for my departure point and destination. This tells me the type of flight to expect: IFR in VFR conditions or IFR in IFR conditions. In the morning I check TWC again and then call DUAT for a complete briefing.

I like DUAT for several reasons. First, I can get in and out of it quickly if all I need is an update on current weather and forecasts, while I might spend 10 minutes on the phone just waiting for an FSS specialist to answer. I can get hard copy of the weather to take with me and refer to later. And I can get much more weather information from DUAT than from flight service, only because it would take too long for a briefer to give me the sequences and forecasts that I can save in just seconds on the computer.

Many pilots have problems with DUAT, as they've been getting their briefings over the phone for so long, they've forgotten how to read coded weather. Many new pilots learn to call flight service and know little about reading weather, never mind interpreting it. The DUAT services will decode weather for you, but they generate a long ribbon of paper.

Weather is a tough subject to learn because it is highly technical. Even the experts don't always forecast it accurately. How are you expected to best the experts? You don't have to. All you need is the ability to take the information presented and decide whether it's possible to make the proposed trip safely. After all, the FARs make you, not the FSS specialist, responsible for the decisions made regarding a flight.

## Personal minimums

Establishing personal limitations helps you make decisions. For example, let's assume the lowest weather acceptable to you for an approach is 600 overcast and 2 miles. If the body of the forecast for your destination and the surrounding area is 100 obscured and a half-mile for the entire day, you won't be going anyway.

There's a lot more to making weather decisions, though. Icing, thunderstorms, turbulence, wind shear, heavy rain, fog and other weather phenomena must be considered. Whether you get your information from an FSS briefer or DUAT, you must have the knowledge to use it and to make an informed decision. Let's look at an IFR briefing and see how to make sense of it.

## Standard briefing

The standard briefing begins with a synopsis intended to give you an idea of where the weather systems are. It's much easier to watch a television weather broadcast or The Weather Channel to get a visual picture. Sometimes the briefer will read the synopsis in the area forecast and you won't recognize the stations or areas.

Viewing the fronts, lows and highs on a map allows you to picture how they might impact your route. Usually, hazardous weather is covered near the beginning of the briefing in case you make an early decision not to go. For example, if you can't fly around thunderstorms or can't find an alternate route around icing conditions, the briefer would prefer to go on to the next call. This is where you must be alert and ask for additional information or you might cancel a trip that could have gone.

I've had briefers stop after giving me the hazardous weather, expecting me to say I'd wait for another day. When I asked them to continue, they did, but grudgingly. I simply needed more information before making a decision.

Next are the current weather conditions followed by the forecasts. If your departure or destination doesn't report, the briefer will refer to other terminals in the area for current and forecast weather, and lacking that, the area forecast.

## Review alternate routes

The briefer should suggest alternate routings, if necessary, to get around weather you might not want to fly through. I've found most of the time, I have to ask for this information. If thunderstorms are near your departure route, the briefer can look at radar and tell you what's out there. Ask if there's a way around the weather, but keep in mind when you get in the air ATC might not have the airspace available you want to fly through. A phone call to the tower or approach control before takeoff might be in order, especially if you don't have weather radar.

Finally, the briefer checks the winds aloft and notams. Many pilots don't pay close attention to the notams, and when they get to their destination they find the ILS they were planning to use is out of service. That's where DUAT is helpful since you get notams for your entire route, and you can print them out. If a change of destination is necessary, you can scan the listing you already have.

Remember, you only get unpublished notams from DUAT and an FSS briefer only gives unpublished notams in a standard briefing. Ask the briefer if you want him/her to review published notams.

## Review the data

You've now spent 15 to 20 minutes on the phone or the computer (the format of the DUAT briefing is similar) collecting the weather information. What's the next step? If the weather is VFR with no hazardous weather along the route, go ahead and file your flight plan. If it's IFR, review everything you have before making a decision.

Some questions you should ask yourself are:

1. Is the weather forecast to be above my personal minimums for the period I'll be in the air? This includes takeoff, en route, and destination weather, as you might need to land early.

2. How old are the forecasts? If new ones will be issued soon, wait for them. The older a forecast is the more likely it will be wrong. You might takeoff and check the weather along the route only to find the new forecasts are much worse than the old ones.

3. Do I have a legal alternate and how sure am I the forecast for the alternate is accurate? The age of the forecast applies here as well.

4. What are the surface winds forecast to be? Will the approach I'm expecting be available with these winds or will I have to do another? Can I circle to land safely if necessary? I once flew with a Citation captain who was determined to land straight-in after a downwind NDB approach. The wind behind us was strong, he was too high and his airspeed too fast to land from the approach. He was below circling

minimums when he made the decision to land in the other direction. He lost his bearings while maneuvering and landed on a runway with a 90-degree crosswind, although I warned him we weren't landing on the correct runway.

5. Can I safely navigate around hazardous weather? In the summer, air mass thunderstorms are usually scattered while severe weather along a front can cover large areas. Avoid weather systems if you don't have radar or other storm detection equipment. In the winter pay close attention to the temperatures in the winds aloft forecasts and the freezing level forecasts in the icing airmets. If you don't have the proper de-ice or anti-ice equipment, and you can't stay clear of icing conditions, DON'T GO!

6. How will the winds aloft affect my flight? Will they slow me down to the point where completing the flight could be questionable? Will I still have my alternate fuel available? Should I make a fuel stop along the way?

7. How do I feel about this flight? Good, I can hack it. There's nothing here I haven't dealt with before. Or, uncertain, I just don't know. There seems to be weather out there and I don't know if I'm prepared for it. If there's any doubt in your mind about your ability to complete the flight, DON'T GO!

A couple of years ago, I took off from Oshkosh IFR after waiting four hours for a clearance. Just west of the airport were thundershowers, but to the east the weather was hot and hazy. I dropped a friend off at Kalamazoo and then proceeded to the Detroit area. When I was over Lake Michigan, I could see that cumulus clouds would be building into thunderstorms over the next hour or so.

A friend of mine was in the lineup at Oshkosh and received his clearance about an hour behind me. He got all the way up to the number one position, took another look at the weather that was now between his departure point and home and decided not to go. He called me that night and told me he would be coming home the next day, after the weather cleared. I told him he had made the right decision, but he didn't have to be told that.

## Forecast vs. reality

When you get airborne, always be alert for anything that wasn't in the forecast. For instance, a front that picks up steam and moves faster than forecast could have more severe weather in it than earlier forecasts indicated. If you're flying toward it, expecting to get to your destination before the weather, you might be in for a big surprise.

Keep abreast of the current conditions using Flight Watch or a regular FSS frequency. If you see something you don't like, find out what's going on. Then, make a safe decision. Should I keep going, land and wait out the weather, or turn around and go back? Don't delay the decision any longer than necessary.

When I first started flying IFR, there were many flight service stations around and the briefers could take their time, helping you learn about the weather as you got your briefing. With the regional flight service stations, everything's changed. You don't get to visit FSSs anymore because they are too widely scattered around the country. I see more automation coming and pilots will need to learn how to read coded weather and interpret it for themselves.

## Publications to study

The government publishes two good books on weather. The first is *Aviation Weather*, which describes weather phenomena for pilots. The second is *Aviation Weather Services* which details the services available to pilots and includes descriptions of the various codes and their meanings. This one is a must for pilots using DUAT.

Most pilots have problems with weather interpretation because they don't devote the time necessary to learn a this complicated subject. The next time you call for a briefing, know exactly what information you need to make a good decision. The best it can do is save your life. The worst it can do is eliminate guessing whether you're going to make it to your destination.

*Everybody knows that weather forecasts are not all that accurate, even though they're a lot better then they used to be. They may get better still, though there's increasing sentiment among scientists and mathematicians that weather may be so complex and delicate a system that it cannot be predicted very far into the future no matter how good our models or how capable our computers are (it's a fairly new concept called chaos theory).*

*Forecasts are particularly suspect when the weather is unsettled, which of course is exactly when instrument pilots must rely on them the most. It pays to be very skeptical when it comes to any sort of prognostication regarding weather systems.*

*Brian Jacobson continues now with a close look at forecasts, and tells of some first-hand experience with some that didn't work out as they were supposed to.*

## Beware of Forecasts

The trip from Providence, RI to Hilton Head, SC was uneventful. The Cessna 402 ran perfectly and the summer weather (a typical hazy, sunny day) was as forecast. I dropped off some golfers for a week on the links and prepared to return home. After refueling the aircraft I called flight service to recheck the weather. The visibility was three to five miles in haze, but otherwise satisfactory for the flight home. The forecast for Norfolk, Virginia (my fuel stop) and Providence was for VFR conditions well into the evening.

Halfway through the two-hour flight to Norfolk I called Flight Watch for an update. The specialist surprised me when he said everything along the coast up to Atlantic City, New Jersey was below minimums. He said it had started at sundown (about 45 minutes earlier) and that ceilings and visibilities were dropping rapidly. Both Atlantic City and Philly were VFR and the forecasts suggested they'd stay that way, although he did add, "But what's going to happen is anybody's guess."

I figured I'd have an hour of fuel remaining at Atlantic City, so instead of trying to find an airport inland that was open I changed my destination to Atlantic City, with Philadelphia as the alternate. I checked the weather twice en route and it was still VFR.

## Murphy intervened

Mr. Murphy is always one to be wary of, though. When the center handed me off to Atlantic City Approach I was expecting an easy approach and landing, until the controller told me the weather was deteriorating rapidly. It dropped to 1200 overcast and three miles in the time it took to switch from ATIS to approach control. As I was setting up for the ILS, the controller told me the airport was now 500 overcast and one mile.

A commuter flight transiting the Atlantic City area asked the controller for Philadelphia weather. Philadelphia was down to 100 obscured and one-eighth mile in fog. The commuter captain decided to land at Atlantic City.

I wondered if there was anyplace to go if I didn't make it into Atlantic City, but didn't have the time to go off the frequency to call flight service. So, I asked the controller if he could tell me how far inland I had to go before it was VFR. After a minute or so he came back and told me Reading and Lancaster, Pennsylvania were VFR or I could go anywhere up into the New York City area.

Some quick figuring told me whichever I chose would take 30 minutes to get to and leave me with 30 minutes of fuel. While this wasn't a great situation, it would have to do. Just inside the marker, the controller told me the weather was now 100 obscured and one-quarter mile visibility with an RVR of 1800 feet (the minimum for the approach). At minimums I saw the approach lights and a couple seconds later, the runway. The commuter landed behind me and the airport went below minimums. I was happy to get in and I'm sure the commuter captain was also.

As it turned out, had I missed the approach, I could have made it into any of the New York City airports as they remained open for a few hours longer. Overnight the entire East Coast, from Maine to South Carolina, went zero-zero and it was three days before the heavy fog lifted.

That flight taught me a valuable lesson. Weather forecasts are, as the word implies, forecasts. The meteorologist uses the best information available and if that information is neither current nor complete, the accuracy of the forecast suffers. The meteorologist's skill and knowledge of scientific principles associated with weather phenomena also impacts the accuracy of forecasts.

## IFR not easy to predict

How accurate are forecasts? A forecast for good weather, with visibilities better than three miles, is likely to be more accurate than a forecast for IFR conditions. Why? It's much more difficult to predict weather phenomena close to the surface with accuracy. Most of the time IFR forecasts include several variables to cover any possibilities that might arise.

For example, suppose your destination is a fictitious airport called Selmel Municipal. The forecast for the next five hours is 800 overcast and three miles, with an occasional ceiling of 600 and one mile in rain, and a chance of 200 obscured and a half-mile in fog. The National Weather Service says that when occasional prefixes a ceiling and/or visibility in a forecast there's a greater than 50 percent chance it will occur, but for less than one half of the forecast period. Chance suggests a 30 to 50 percent probability, and slight chance means a 10 to 20 percent probability the associated phenomena will occur.

While all this makes sense to the meteorologist preparing the forecast, what does it mean to the pilot who must interpret it? To me it means don't turn your back on the weather. Like the FSS briefer told me, "What's going to happen is anybody's guess."

What if your personal minimums are 600 and one for the ILS at your destination and you get the previous forecast? Would you consider the chance of 200 obscured and a half-mile in fog limiting? That, of course, is for you to decide, but there are a couple of ways to approach this forecast.

## Wait for the new one

First, the older the forecast is the greater the chance it will be incorrect.

So, if you're looking at a newly issued forecast, for the next five hours it's more likely to be correct than one nearing the end of its period. You should consider waiting for the next issuance before making your go/no-go decision if a new forecast is due soon.

Forecasts for IFR conditions are most reliable during the first few hours if there's a front, low or other weather system in the area. While there are times I can remember when IFR weather was not as bad as the forecast suggested, most of the time (when dealing with low ceilings and visibilities) it'll be worse than forecast.

If you limit yourself to 600 and one for the Selmel ILS, and the forecast is the same as the example above, the weather will probably be closer to 600 and one; right at your personal minimum. Be alert for that 200 obscured and half-mile sneaking up on you also. You should have a suitable alternate picked out with a forecast that is better than your personal minimum, if you choose to fly the trip.

Another way to approach this forecast is to use the Weather Service's forecasting probabilities. For instance, if the body of the Selmel forecast is good for five hours, after which a change in the weather will occur, then Selmel could be 600 and one for as much as 50 percent of that time. Which 50 percent, though, is anybody's guess.

Also, there's a 30 to 50 percent chance that Selmel will be 200 obscured and a half-mile in fog when you get there. When you're considering whether or not to fly, remember the weather is likely to be worse than the body of the forecast suggests. Again, you'll need a suitable alternate you can be confident will remain above your personal minimums.

## Get continuous updates

En route, get updates on the weather at Selmel, the surrounding area and your alternate. Let's consider what could happen if Selmel went below your personal minimums and there was little promise it would improve before you got there. Suppose flight service says your alternate, Wefax (75 miles from Selmel), is close to its forecast.

Since you want to keep all your options open, you ask for the weather at Repip (only 15 miles from Selmel), which is forecasting the same weather, but is reporting 900 overcast and four miles. If you have enough fuel you could continue toward Selmel with three options.

First, you could land at Selmel if it improved before you got there. Second, if Selmel didn't improve, but Repip stayed the same or above your personal minimums, you could land there and at least be close to Selmel. Third, if Selmel didn't improve and Repip went down as well, you could proceed to Wefax (your alternate).

What if you had a three-hour flight and the new forecasts were due to be issued in two hours? Remember, old forecasts are more likely to be incorrect. I suggest picking an airport (approximately two hours along your route) that can be used in case the new forecasts indicate deteriorating conditions for your destination and alternate. If the new forecasts are bleak and the weather is deteriorating, you could land and wait or, if good weather is behind you, return to home base.

## Be skeptical about amendments

You should evaluate very carefully a forecast that's been amended more than once. An amendment is issued if a meteorologist finds the weather isn't living up to the original forecast. This happens a lot in the morning when fog is slower to lift than the person originating the forecast expected. When a forecast is amended, it usually reflects the current weather, plus the meteorologist's new estimate for when clearing can be expected.

A forecast amended more than once indicates a lack of understanding by the meteorologist of the weather phenomena, but it isn't necessarily the meteorologists fault. For example, if a system that's supposed to move through an area slowly suddenly picks up speed, you have a whole different set of circumstances and weather.

What would you do if Selmel's forecast had been amended three or four times? The latest amendment probably isn't going to be any more accurate than the last. The best plan is to delay your departure until you get a clear indication of what the weather is going to do. If the latest amendment simply mirrors what's currently happening, it really isn't a forecast.

When ground fog is the culprit, you can use current reports as an indication that improvement is beginning. For example, I flew my Cessna 172 from Howell, Michigan to Dayton, Ohio. My departure and destination airports were fog-bound and the forecast amendments were coming faster than flight service could keep up with them. About an hour after my scheduled departure, Toledo and Dayton started to improve. As soon as I had ILS minimums at both of them, I was on my way. When I reached the Dayton area, my destination was VFR.

## Consider the options

When flying a single-engine airplane IFR, keep several things in mind when reviewing the weather and forecasts for your flight. First, make sure there are places to go along the entire route in the event you have a problem. For example, if your vacuum pump takes a holiday halfway, get on the ground immediately. Flying partial panel isn't something any of us do often enough and trying to make it all the way to your destination without gyros would be foolhardy.

Losing a vacuum pump in a twin, with a pump on each engine or in a single with an auxiliary vacuum source wouldn't necessarily be a serious problem, but if you've only got one pump a failure could ruin your whole day.

The day I took off in my C-172, Toledo and Dayton were above ILS minimums and continued to improve as I flew south. I could have landed at either airport if necessary. To take off with no assurance the weather is above your personal minimums along the route is asking for trouble. Many singles and some light twins don't have a very good range. Sometimes finding a suitable alternate can be a problem, especially if your destination isn't near a large terminal. It's tempting to use a forecast that's near the end of its term instead of waiting for the new one to come out. Often, when the weather is correctly forecast to be IFR, the next terminal forecasts will predict lower conditions than the earlier one. Your alternate might not be an alternate any longer.

## Find a close-by alternate

If you're planning a three-hour IFR flight in a four-hour airplane, you need a good alternate within 15 minutes of your destination, including time to make an approach. If you can't find an airport and alternate where you can stop and refuel along the way, don't attempt the flight. While it's possible to be perfectly legal, it doesn't mean you're perfectly safe.

Taking time to examine the forecasts thoroughly and locate airports along the route where the weather is expected to remain above your personal minimums is nothing more than finding yourself a way out. A good instrument pilot always has an alternate plan in mind in case things don't work as expected.

Forecasting weather isn't an easy job and, like most other things in life, is never perfect. Review the forecasts and assume they'll be worse than expected. Play the what if game before you launch. Never consider the forecasts to be gospel. The first time you do Mr. Murphy will be waiting to step in, sneer in your face and cause trouble you could have avoided.

*Up until now we've been going over various questions to ask yourself when deciding whether to fly, techniques to get the best information, and so forth.*

*But, the bottom line is that you should have a clear idea of what it will take to keep you from flying, or to turn around if things start going wrong. If you define your personal limits ahead of time, making the decision to quit will be easier than when you're under pressure. For example, set a simple limit, such as: "I absolutely, positively will not fly if the forecast is for ceilings less than 200 feet above the decision height."*

*Then, when it's late Sunday night and you have to be back at work Monday morning you can eliminate the effects of fatigue or the "get-home-itis" factor by simply checking the forecast. If the numbers don't meet your standard, don't fly.*

*We've asked some of our contributors and acquaintances to tell us about their personal limits and rules.*

## What Makes You Say No?

If there's anything nice about the weather in the Northeast, it's the variety. During the spring, we can count on an interesting selection of rain and low-ceilings, a little ice and around March on, some nasty frontal thunderstorms. Forget the ice and thunder for a minute, let's talk about those low ceilings.

Around here, a ground-hugging layer of stratus is perfect for picking up a little actual and flying some approaches to minimums, assuming, of course, that the very notion of going out in such weather intentionally doesn't strike you as lunacy.

Which brings us to the point of this section. About half the pilots we know think nothing of charging off into low ceilings just for the sport of it; the other half won't even entertain the thought of it, or so they say. But we know from having flown with pilots of all ilks that few hard rules govern judgment.

We've seen a pilot grandly pronounce on one day that he always cancels when there's ice in the pireps and then blithely launch into those very conditions the next day. This confirms what most of us probably know: the go/no-go judgment is a moving target.

## Bob Gardner
## ATP-CFII, Former DE
## 7000 Hours

My philosophy has always been that a newly-minted instrument pilot has learned two things: first, how to control and navigate an airplane without visual references and second, that doing so is hard work. So my first question is always "What are the tops?"

Then, depending on whether I'm going west to east over the mountains or north to south down toward California, I want to know how much of a gap exists between the bases of the lowest layer and the terrain. Heading down Interstate 5, I would probably accept an average ceiling of about 500 feet, while going over the mountains I want at least 1500 feet at Stampede Pass, which is a reporting station in the Cascade Mountains.

I wouldn't take off into a ceiling of less than 400 feet, no matter what. If I do come gliding out of the cloud bases behind a windmilling prop, I'd like at least that much opportunity to choose something soft or inexpensive to hit. In a training context, I don't want to give a student the impression that low-ceiling departures are the norm.

Taking a student into an area where the weather is at minimums or below, however, is a different story. I loathe and despise "vision restricting devices" and happily leave mine in the flight case if the weather cooperates. One real missed approach is worth a dozen "take-off-the-hood-and-land" scenarios. A brief glimpse of the runway while going around is frosting on the cake.

We have three airways between Seattle and eastern Washington, with MEAs of 8000, 10000 and 12000 feet. I won't fly a Cessna 172 or equivalent IFR on V120, with its 12000-foot MEA because Center is going to put me at 13,000 feet and I'm going to run out of performance. I'll usually opt for V2, with its low MEA. North and south, the MEAs don't get too demanding until you get to southern Oregon; I can re-evaluate the situation by the time I get that far south.

I flatter myself that I know enough about conditions conducive to structural icing that I can do my own forecasting and safely ignore the general warnings. If there is a pirep of icing, I try to relate it to my research of the weather charts, and if the pirep confirms what the charts indicate I'll stay on the ground. This is fairly uncommon, however.

Coming back from eastern Washington in the winter, I know that the whole airplane will be cold, and that a normal descent through the wet clouds that live on the western slopes of the Cascades will turn it into an ice cube. In those conditions, I ask for vectors well west of Seattle before letting down.

If I can climb through the freezing level to on-top in an area where I can get back down again reasonably safely, I'll work out a deal with ATC to accomplish that. Almost everything I need is available from DUAT without calling up charts, although the possibility of icing means downloading as much of the four-panel Composite Moisture Stability Chart as is available, plus a couple of constant pressure charts.

The one important question that DUAT can't answer easily is "Where do I go to find VFR?" The area forecast is too general in nature for that, so I check with the FSS. The synopsis tells me about the stability of the air mass and the winds aloft forecasts give me a general idea of where the wind is coming from. I know where the sources of moisture and the mountains are, so I can get a fairly good idea of where moist, rising air is in relation to where I'm going.

A forecast of embedded thunderstorms is enough to keep me on the ground. "Taking a look" with TRWs hidden in a stratus layer is not too smart, but that condition is about the only thing that would prevent me from taking a look. It's important to note here that the folks at Seattle Center and tracon are the most cooperative in the nation, and of course they have more airspace to work with than the east coast controllers.

I was 40 years old before I started giving instrument instruction and flying serious instruments. Before that, it must have been clean living that kept me alive, because looking back on my first couple of hundred hours of IFR I really didn't know what I was doing. "If I knew then what I know now..." if you know what I mean.

Of course, every instructor is motivated to put out students with better preparation than he or she got. It's paradoxical that as the years go by and I get more experience I grow more reluctant to stick my neck out. Saying "no" is much easier now than when I was building hours toward my ATP. Part of that has to do with what little measure of notoriety I have gained through writing. I don't want my students or readers to find my name in an accident report and say "How could Bob have done something as dumb as that?"

## Chuck Kissner
## Private Pilot, ASMEL
## 3000 Hours

Life used to be so simple. Twenty years ago, if there was weather, if a rental plane wasn't available, if there was a party on the horizon, or if I was short of cash, I didn't fly. I amassed a grand total of about 250 hours and often wondered why I got a pilot's license in the first place.

With more flying experience, my limits seemed to stretch. Finally, during a serious episode of scud running, I thought about all the things that I hadn't yet experienced in my brief life. I vowed that if I survived, I would forever change my attitude about flying and my own limits.

Most of my flying now is for business. I'm based in California and with most of my business on the east coast and in the Midwest, I generally fly transcontinental routes in the U.S. and Canada in my Malibu. This amounts to 400 hours a year and it subjects me to just about every conceivable kind of weather, along with the continuing potential to test both my limits and those of the airplane.

I believe that each flight has a number of elements which can become weak links. My overall philosophy is to identify those weak links and employ strategies to minimize them. By far, the best way to do this is to have alternatives for everything, not just weather alternates. This eliminates the pressure to press on with a plan that seemed wonderful at one time, but suddenly doesn't look too great. I assume that *something* will go wrong on every flight. It could be the weather, the aircraft, me, my business appointment, anything.

I try to build flexibility into my business schedule. But I usually don't have that option, so I always carry a set of airline tickets for *every* leg of the trip so I can reasonably keep the schedule I've set. In the middle of a trip, if the weather is so lousy that I consider it unacceptable to fly myself, I can always go commercial and pick up the airplane later.

Having alternatives also includes alternate routing. If I'm traveling from San Francisco to Chicago, I've found that I can go north or south of course by 200 miles to avoid buildups, and not significantly affect my schedule. I've learned not to be too intent on cutting a few miles off the route when there are thunderstorms to contend with. At best, the time savings are minimal and besides, I'd rather arrive late than stressed out from picking my way through cells.

I'm truly obsessed with the mechanical status of the airplane. I won't begin a long trip unless everything works and I try to keep things working during the entire trip. Besides the safety and legal aspects, when something breaks, it devastates the schedule. Also, staying ahead of mechanical problems is important because they tend to accumulate during a trip until I have to get things fixed at an inopportune time. That violates my requirement to always have alternatives.

I normally fly back to California from the east coast in a day but I won't do that without a copilot. I prefer to have a copilot for the rest of the trip as well. If I can't get a copilot, I'll stop overnight and do the trip in two legs. I've discovered over the years that there are lots of very qualified pilots (mostly bored flight instructors) who jump at the chance to make one of these flights. It's great to have the company and I find that we learn from each other on every trip.

The chance of having no significant weather on coast-to-coast trips is about as likely as a Cessna 152 getting priority treatment at JFK at 6:00 p.m. next Friday. I won't normally fly a scheduled long-distance business trip without pressurization, de-ice, and weather detection equipment. Failure of the weather radar or de-ice are grounds for trip cancellation.

RNAV is a no-go item, too. Most of the places I fly in the U.S. have airports reachable from FL240-250, given the glide range of a Malibu. I want to be able to find the airport and RNAV is invaluable in doing so.

I also practice power-off approaches, including ILSs, to make the odds more favorable.

Even with operating equipment, I will go far out of my way to avoid significant weather. If I'm tired and don't have a top-notch copilot and can't avoid operating in areas of thunderstorms, I will delay or cancel a trip. It takes a lot of work to circumvent thunderstorms, and the consequences of error are too exciting for me to imagine.

Even with the de-ice equipment, I try to avoid any ice heavier than light. That's because I assume that the deice stuff could fail at any time, especially the prop heat, which has been known to break a wire just when I need it.

Just encountering ice, though, won't cause me to cancel a flight. Neither will low ceilings. I fly hard IMC enough to stay proficient and have reasonable faith in the aircraft. I will not take off, however, if ceilings are below minimums at the departure airport nor will I try a "look-see" approach at an airport reporting below minimums. It's legal to try, but I figure it's just not worth the risk of an accident, especially considering the ramifications of shooting an approach where the reported weather suggests that my decision to land was questionable.

That takes care of the explicit rules. But there's one that's even more important. It's instinct. Although many pilots think it's baloney, I've learned to listen to it. The most dramatic example occurred in 1987, when I was to fly a rental aircraft from San Jose to Los Angeles.

I woke up on that clear Thanksgiving morning looking forward to a beautiful flight down the California coast. But something just didn't feel right. I really wanted to go, but finally called up and canceled. A couple of other pilots took the airplane next (a round trip to Southern California). A cylinder cracked, resulting in a fire in the engine compartment. The crash killed one pilot and seriously burned the other.

I continue to look for ways to make my flying useful and safe. Twenty years ago, the no-go decision was made far more often than the go. The reverse is true today and I feel safer for knowing my limits and sticking to them. I consider it a form of insurance against two big killers: complacency and misjudgment.

## Martha Morris
## ATP-CFII
## King Air Pilot
## 5300 Hours

Flying paying passengers in an all-weather airplane like the King Air, we seldom say no. Either by personal choice or regulation, we occasionally venture out when other pilots choose to stay on the ground. That's a fact of life that fly-for-hire pilots have to get used to and there's no question it can complicate the yes-no decision.

We fly under both Part 91 and Part 135 and this can impose a certain schizophrenia on judgment and decision-making. Under 135, some operating limitations are written in stone; no takeoffs in less than one mile of visibility, no approach attempts when the weather is reported below minimums. Yet under 91, we can takeoff and shoot approaches in any kind of weather we want. Same airplane; same weather; different rules.

On 91 flights, we have taken off when the weather was reported sky-obscured, visibility zero. The airlines were paralyzed. We had some forward visibility down the runway and—our personal, worst-case rule—we had good VFR weather within a half hour flying time on one engine. We popped out on top at 2500 feet and continued on our way. Was that risky? A little, perhaps. But we flew the trip because we knew we could do it safely.

When it comes to approaches, we generally follow the Part 135 limits; no approaches commenced unless reported weather is at minimums. None of this look-see nonsense for us. If the destination is below minimums, we say no. Period.

Concerning ice, my personal view is that just because the aircraft is certified for known ice, that's no reason to put it to the test. We scan the pireps for ice and try to avoid it as best we can. When we find it, we usually try to climb out of it and it's nice to have the power to do that. I just feel awful hearing all those single-engine guys (cargo dogs, I assume) struggling along at the MEA in icing conditions. I know what kind of schedule pressure these pilots are subjected to; it's much harder for them to say no and in a lot of cases, they have few options because of equipment limitations.

Thunderstorms are a way of life in the southwest. The biggest problem for us seems to be wind shear and blowing dust during takeoff and landing. If a takeoff looks chancy, we'll simply wait it out; conditions are apt to improve quickly and saving a few minutes is just not worth the risk. In the air, we'll try to pick our way around cells with the radar and Stormscope. The limiting factor is fuel. When the cells get bad enough (too big and too wide) we call it quits and land.

In flying this heavy-duty IFR—low takeoffs, ice and thunder—currency is essential. I fly 30 to 60 hours a month, plus I attend simulator-based recurrent training every six months. Maintenance is critical, too. Whether 91 or 135, if it ain't right, we fix it or we don't go. No tough decision there.

Experience is a funny thing in that the more you have, the less likely you are to take chances. In my personal flying (mostly Cessna 182s here in the southwest), my rule is to not fly into clouds. It seems to be my luck that there's always ice or convective activity out here and I get my fill of that at work. Besides, I feel positively naked without the radar and de-ice.

Does that mean that I think venturing into IMC in a single is nuts? Not at all. I only wish the clouds in Arizona were benign enough—meaning no cells and no ice—to do it safely.

## Klaus Kraemer
## Private Pilot
## 500 Hours

Like everyone else, I've made the no decision a couple of times, with and without passengers aboard. But I have also decided a couple times (without passengers) not to say no. And every time I did that, I gained from the experience.

I go into clouds not because I have to get somewhere; I leave that to the Part 121 drivers. I fly IFR primarily to *learn how to fly* IFR. I remember the enormous rush of adrenaline when I first dove into a stratus deck with an instructor in the right seat. You never get that experience from flying under the hood.

Okay, so I'm one of those pilots who seek out IMC. I check the weather to see where it's bad and sometimes I go there on purpose. I don't consider this risky as long as there is no pressure to complete the approach. I don't use the airplane to make business appointments; I don't carry passengers for hire.

I'm not afraid to fly an approach to minimums. I've done it intentionally and will continue to do so. How else to get proficient at flying in real weather? I believe it's safe to fly an approach even when the weather is below minimums for training and practice, as long as you're absolutely primed to miss and go somewhere else where the weather is good.

Takeoff minimums? I'm still figuring that out. Where I'm based in California, we rarely get enough weather to constitute real minimums of any kind. So for now, if the weather is good enough to allow a VFR return to my homebase (Reid-Hillview) or an ILS to San Jose, five miles away, I'll consider going. Otherwise, no thanks.

Ice? Never had it. When it's in the forecast or pireps, I fly around it or under it. Or I don't go. Ice is a pretty clear no-go to me.

When I was a teenager and couldn't swim, I decided to go out with friends and plunge myself into the wet anyway. Some kind soul observed my subsequent struggle and pushed me ashore. I survived, as you may have surmised, but I still can't swim. Does that tell you about ignorance as a teacher and motivator?

I truly believe that if you want to improve yourself, you've got to push beyond the limits of your current knowledge. Just how far to go, that's the question. If you ignore what you've learned and abide by the rules of other pilots instead of developing your own, you could get into hot water. But if you haven't pushed, at least a little, you haven't learned anything.

## J. Ross Russo
## ATP-CFII, F-16 Pilot
### 6500 Hours

Most of my aviation education has come as a result of the error and trial method. Some pilot makes an error, the NTSB conducts the trial, and I read about it. What better way to learn than to have someone else pick up the tuition?

One thing's for sure: running into trouble is synonymous with running out of options. Those are nice words and they're easy to agree with when you're sitting in your easy chair reading about personal limits. But when you're enmeshed in the pressure of everyday life, it's not always easy to act rationally.

The Air Force makes it a little easier for its pilots. The regulations are both more numerous and restrictive than in civil aviation. There's usually a disinterested party perched on a loftier branch of the decision tree. Additionally, weather minimums are based on pilot experience and currency. They may be as high as 700-foot ceilings and visibilities of two miles. Even the best pilots in the squadron are usually limited to 300 and 1.

I understand the logic of this. The Air Force has awfully expensive equipment flown by some relatively inexperienced pilots. That said, I don't necessarily believe that such conservative minimums should apply when I'm flying Part 91. My speeds are slower and I usually have a much greater fuel reserve than the average fighter pogue. As long as turbulence, darkness or fatigue don't figure into the equation, I won't hesitate to shoot an approach to minimums. But if I have to juggle anything extra, then I bump up my personal mins. I like to have at least 500 feet of good air between published minimums and reported weather.

Below minimums? Not for me, thanks. The trap of the Part 91 look-see has snagged too many pilots. I'll look elsewhere.

Flying in Florida, I've found that three things make me say no: fog, ice, and thunderstorms. Fog is the worst. There's just no way to win against it, especially at night. If I see a combination of high pressure, light winds and a close temperature/dewpoint spread, I go to plan B. If the vis goes below minimums, I'm outta there or it's a flat no in the first place.

I feel the same way about takeoffs below Part 91 landing minimums. Sure, some instructors feel it's beneficial to show the student a "real" ITO, but the risk/benefit ratio just doesn't hack the program. Same for practice approaches when the weather's zero-zero. These are the things simulators were designed for.

Ice is something I'm not very familiar with. Consequently, I avoid it. Still, I've flown in ice and have accepted it. Specifically, I was cruising through Florida and Alabama at 14,000 feet, picking up light rime. There was plenty of warm air beneath me so I wasn't particularly worried. Give me reports of icing at low altitude though, the kind of stuff that I'd have to fly through on departure or during an approach, and I'm a dot. Confirmed ice at low altitudes is a definite no for me. By the way, I always carry a large lantern to check the wings during night flights. I also use it to take a look at the engines on a twin.

# Electronic
# Weather Avoidance

For the most part, pilots use their intelligence and judgement to keep clear of weather. We gather forecast and "current" ground observation information from a variety of sources and make decisions based on it. It's all a very indirect process.

There are, however, a handful of tools a pilot can use to see what the weather is doing right here, right now. One is airborne radar, which relatively few can afford. Another on-board instrument is the storm detector (e.g. Stormscope), which can easily prove to be the cheapest insurance a pilot has if it's used properly. Lastly, there's ATC, which can display precipitation, albeit in a limited fashion.

In this chapter we'll look at using Stormscopes, airborne and ATC radar to keep clear of bad weather.

## Using Airborne Radar

While interviewing for a corporate Turbo-Commander job a couple of years ago, the owner of the company asked a pilot we know if he'd ever flown through a thunderstorm. He answered truthfully that he hadn't. He admits to anyone who asks he's come close a few times, but he's never mixed it up with these pervasive harbingers of Mother Nature.

From the incredulous look on the interviewer's face the pilot knew he'd lost the job. The interview went on about other subjects and twice more he asked, "You've never flown through a thunderstorm?" When he asked for the third time, the pilot wondered about his preoccupation.

"Is that why you are looking for a new pilot?" he asked. He couldn't believe any pilot would intentionally fly through a thunderstorm to get his passengers to their destination. As a rule, any sane individual should recognize the need for steering clear of these weather monsters.

"I've had some problems with my present pilot," the interviewer stated, "and that's why I'm looking for a new one. But every pilot I've ever hired has admitted flying through thunderstorms on occasion."

The interview ended shortly afterward and the pilot was right: he didn't get the job. The man hired a pilot who had little turbo-prop experience and none in the Commander. But, he must have admitted to having flown through at least one thunderstorm.

## ATC radar

Back in the early and mid-1970s, controllers had more airspace to work with since there were fewer airplanes in the air. Not only that, but the type of radar approach controllers used in those days displayed weather better than the current generation does. It wasn't unusual to call an approach controller ahead of the route of flight to ask for the best way around the weather. Sometimes pilots would even descend into approach control airspace so they could get vectors around weather. The controllers were very helpful about weather avoidance.

It's not unusual today for a controller to ask a pilot for information from airborne radar in order to compare it with the ATC display. we've also heard controllers issue weather advisories to pilots with the caution, "But I don't know what the intensity of it is." We've had controllers tell us we were about to fly into weather when there wasn't any.

## New gear requires training

As the price of airborne weather radar came down, it showed up in the radio stacks of light twins and even some high-performance singles. It has greatly enhanced our ability to maneuver around weather, but weather radar is a sophisticated piece of equipment that must be used properly to be of any benefit. A pilot who just turns it on and waits for it to display bad weather with little or no knowledge of how it works is inviting disaster.

For example, you're in the clouds watching thunderstorms build ahead on radar. Since radar displays rainfall intensities, you note the red spots (high intensity returns) are increasing in size. As you get closer to the heavy rain, you turn left toward an area of green or light rainfall. You figure you can fly through there and be in the clear on the other side in a few miles.

The ride is smooth as you enter the light rain, but within a couple of miles that changes. Looking over your scope again you see everything in front of you is red blotches. There doesn't appear to be a way through. What happened?

## Shadowing

Not all the signal radiated by the radar transmitter returns to the receiver. Some of it is attenuated or absorbed by the weather itself. In this example, the high intensity rainfall attenuated much of the radar signal and shadowed or masked the ominous cells behind the visible ones. By trying to get through the area of lighter rainfall our pilot got boxed in. Anytime you have an area of light precipitation surrounded by higher intensities, there's a good chance the weather is still building and will fill the area with heavier rainfall.

## Using the tilt

Another problem occurs at higher altitudes, where the moisture in a thunderstorm freezes and doesn't reflect as well. A way around this is to point the antenna down to reflect the warmer precip at lower levels. Depending on your altitude and how many degrees you tilt the antenna down, you might also get a return from the ground that can obscure the true character of the weather.

How you tilt the antenna is critical in any airborne radar system. Zero tilt (the angle at which the antenna is looking straight ahead) varies with different aircraft and at different altitudes.

For example, the power output of any engine will decrease with altitude, which means the attitude required to maintain level flight at high altitudes (how high depends on how your engine is aspirated) will be higher than at a lower altitude. Similarly, the radar antenna, when set at the same tilt used at a lower altitude might be pointed over the horizon instead of straight ahead. You could be flying with your antenna looking over weather in your path and not realize it.

Air-mass thunderstorms that pop up in hot, humid conditions are generally widely scattered and visible to the eye. That makes them easy to get around unless they develop into lines or clusters. The best technique to use in dealing with these is simple avoidance. Keep as much distance between them and your aircraft as possible. One rule-of-thumb in thunderstorm avoidance is to stay at least five miles from the edges of a cell if the temperature is above freezing and ten miles if it's below freezing. Above 25,000 feet never get closer than 20 miles.

Some pilots believe they can use weather radar to get closer to severe weather. Before you allow yourself that luxury, remember, radars aren't infallible. We mentioned shadowing (where the cells in front mask others) making them invisible. You must always be sure you have a way out in case things aren't what you expected when you penetrate weather. Sometimes the only way to do that is to use the radar to take a wide berth of the weather or remain where you can see the cells as you go around them.

## Go out of your way to avoid

Often, especially at lower altitudes, cells will be embedded in the clouds and not visible. If you aren't certain you have a safe buffer between the cells, don't attempt it. Use the radar, instead, to circumnavigate the whole system or land and wait it out.

Weather radars fail on occasion and it might not be apparent because the screen still looks normal. If the transmitter power is weak, for example, the signal reflected back to the antenna might not give you an accurate picture of what is ahead.

Don't rely solely on the radar for your weather avoidance strategy. Listen carefully to others on the frequency. Ask ATC if there are any reports of severe weather ahead. Talk to Flight Watch and ask what the local picture looks like. If you have any doubt about the accuracy or condition of your weather radar, get yourself in a position from which you can see the cells or on the ground where you can wait out the weather and get the radar repaired.

## Terminal areas

Terminal operations are a major concern during severe weather. When using airborne weather radar, you're more likely to continue your approach, departure or landing with the belief you can beat the weather. Your radar only displays precipitation at various intensities. It doesn't show turbulence or wind shear that can accompany these storms and exist some distance from the cell itself. For more on wind shear, see the next chapter and Section Three, Weather Hazards.

## Who's in charge?

One time, we were inbound to Teterboro, New Jersey at 3000 feet with various intensities of weather displayed in all directions. The controller was extremely busy with aircraft wanting to deviate. we had a cell directly in front of us and wanted to turn. The controller refused to answer our call. we kept trying and he finally answered by telling us to remain on course. We told him we were going to turn to avoid the weather that was now five miles away and asked if he would prefer it to the right or left. "If you must turn make it to the left," he replied.

Don't let controllers fly the airplane. If you believe there's threatening weather in front of you, tell ATC what you're going to do if they refuse to allow deviations. You have the sole responsibility for the safety of your flight, and you're within your rights to deviate as necessary to keep yourself out of danger.

If you're operating an airplane with weather radar and have never taken a course on its use, we recommend you do so. You'll learn how it works and, most importantly, how to interpret what you're seeing.

Single-engine airplanes aren't built to withstand the g-forces you can encounter in thunderstorms. Under the right conditions, such as a high speed descent in an area of embedded cells, turbulence and wind shear associated with a cell can be severe enough to do damage. Often, destructive phenomena occur outside the cell itself.

The best way to use airborne radar is as a tool to give you a wide berth around severe weather. Don't be lulled into thinking it'll keep you out of trouble. It won't if you don't understand how it works or how to interpret the display.

*Next we'll hear from bush pilot and contributor Fred Potts on his experiences with the Stormscope.*

## Stormscopes for Weather Avoidance

From a mountain clearing, safely ensconced within a strong and comfortable cabin, a thunderstorm at full throttle is an awesome and beautiful sight. But from a small aircraft in flight, with thunderstorms in all quadrants, the sight loses much of its beauty; and if in IMC with embedded cells, there is no beauty at all.

Thunderstorms are highly developed cumulus clouds (think of them as having an overdose of testosterone), and cumulus clouds, because of their very nature, provide a bumpy ride. In their tops there is often ice, and as they develop they reach a point where precipitation begins. This precipitation is what airborne radar detects; unfortunately, precipitation is not a reliable indicator of turbulence and it is the turbulence in a thunderstorm that can kill us.

This is where the 3M Stormscopes (and Insight's Strike Finder) come into the picture. These instruments detect and analyze the electromagnetic fields produced by lightning through evaluation of their individual signatures, a science known as sferics. And lightning shows a strong correlation to turbulence.

However, to avoid this turbulence, it is necessary to know a bit about the various stages in the life of a thunderstorm, for both radars and

Stormscopes require knowledge and understanding if one is to correctly interpret their subtleties and idiosyncrasies.

Of the various weather mapping instruments available, I've found the 3M Series II Stormscopes to be the easiest to understand and use. In this article I will be focusing primarily on the WX-1000+, the unit I chose for my Turbo Cessna 206. Because the 3M manuals fail to cover the finer points of Stormscope operation, I'll try to rectify this shortcoming by reporting on my own experience with the Series II. It should be noted, however, that the Pilot's Operating Handbook takes precedence over anything written here.

## What the Stormscope sees

Put simply, as cumulus clouds develop in the unstable air, they penetrate the freezing level and the moisture in the updrafts becomes supercooled. These cooler temperatures, combined with the weight of the moisture, create downdrafts. Between the updrafts and downdrafts, an area of convective wind shear develops. Here you will find strong up and downdrafts (often reaching 2,500 to 3,000 feet per minute), possibly severe turbulence, and icing. Because precipitation has usually not yet begun, radar is of little help. However, electrical activity generally has started at this stage, and while the developing thunderstorm is not yet visible to radar, it is visible to devices that map the electromagnetic signals (lightning, either cloud-to-cloud or cloud-to-ground) that these building storms produce.

At the earliest stages of development a light accumulation of discharge points will begin to appear on the Stormscope's CRT. These discharge points represent lightning strikes and are shown in their calculated positions, both by azimuth and distance. (With the Series II Stormscopes, distance accuracy—using verified ground triangulation—has been shown to be within 10 percent.)

At first, there won't be many of these discharge points. If the CLEAR button is used, they will be slow to return. But after a while, they will begin to increase in both number and rate of build-up, taking the form of a small but growing cluster. This growing cluster (a rough indication of the size and shape of the storm) is a clear sign that the cumulus is beginning to mature into a thunderstorm. And it is such clusters that must be avoided.

## Keep your distance

Keep all clusters at least 25 nautical miles from your airplane. This range is outside the safety circle, which is shown on the Stormscope as a solid circle when it's in the 360-degree mode. When using the 120-degree forward display while close to the storm, keep the clusters not only outside the 25-mile safety arc, but outside the 30-degree lines as well. This will not guarantee you a smooth ride, but it will help keep you out of the truly dangerous turbulence.

As the storm matures, the moisture (whether rain, hail, sleet, or snow) becomes heavy enough to fall against the force of the updrafts. This precipitation fuels the downdrafts even more. The storm (which would now be visible on radar if you had it) is moving into its most dangerous phase, and at the surface the downrushing air spreads outward in strong gusts accompanied by a sharp temperature drop.

As the storm gains strength, the discharge points on your CRT will start to scintillate (flicker): their rate of growth and scintillation is an indication of the storm's severity.

If random-appearing discharge points seem to "splatter" around the aircraft symbol with an active cell nearby (perhaps just inside the safety circle), it is an indication that you are much too close to that storm. Immediately turn away. Be aware that any grouping of discharge points within the 25-mile safety circle is cause for concern.

Eventually entropy, the nemesis and fate of all organized matter, catches up with the thunderstorm. As the downdrafts cool the air in the cell, they cut off the flow of heated air to the updraft. This weakens the updraft, and therefore the convective wind shear, and gradually the electromagnetic activity dies down. This signals the oncoming death of the storm. Soon all that will be left are harmless drifting cloud remnants.

On the Stormscope's screen, the strikes will slowly begin to fade, and two to four minutes after the electrical discharges cease, the storm will drop off your CRT. There's often intense rainfall at this stage, but the Stormscope will not show this, just as it does not show the presence of hail, or the various forms of turbulence not associated with electromagnetic discharges.

If you're on top of the situation, you will have been keeping track of the various cells in your vicinity and marking their direction and speed of movement. If you are interested in staying out of the potential drownpour, you will know exactly what area to detour around even though the cluster has disappeared from your CRT.

## Lines and complexes

The above has been a description of a simple airmass thunderstorm and its life-cycle, along with a description of what you are likely to see on a Series II Stormscope's CRT. But, of course, in the real world thunderstorms, being sociable, like company, and so are often found in lines and groups in various stages of growth.

And, while the FAA and NWS classify thunderstorms by six levels (using the precipitation returns from radar, actually an indirect measurement), and meteorologists like to divide them into four general classifications, experienced thunderstorm researchers tend to break them into three classes. Jerry Smith, research pilot for 3M, classifies them as little, medium, and killer. Dennis Newton, in his fine book *Severe Weather Flying,* is a bit more colorful, calling them Baby Bear, Mama Bear, and (the Big Daddy) Papa Bear.

As Newton observes, Papa Bears generally travel in gregarious packs, complete with Mama Bears and Baby Bears, and that would surely seem to be enough of a family get-together for anyone. Yet these family groups also have another offspring, a lovely child we call a tornado.

Radar has a long history behind it, and we have gotten used to spotting tornados by the infamous "hook" return. But the Stormscope's history is far shorter (sferics is, after all, a fairly new science), and the established knowledge base is much smaller. As a result, we must use indirect means to locate tornados when relying on sferics devices, just as radar operators must use indirect means to gauge the strength of a thunderstorm.

Since I have never had the dubious pleasure of seeing a tornado on my Stormscope, I am going to give you the description of someone who has. Jerry Smith, 3M's research pilot, flies thunderstorms for a living, and one night he described to me what a tornado looks like on the Stormscope's CRT. To use his words, "It goes wild." The dots (crosses) are coming in so fast, and the scintillation (flicker) is so severe, that the cluster stands out markedly from the normal clusters.

However, Smith cautions that while all the tornados he has seen produced this very rapid repetition of dots and severe scintillation, he has also seen violent thunderstorms that did the same, even though tornados were not associated with them.

If you see an area on your CRT "going wild," press your CLEAR button. If the pattern snaps right back, perhaps even intensifying, treat it as confirmation of your worst suspicions and do exactly what the primitive reptile brain buried deep within the top of your spinal cord advises. Tornado or not, that's an area to stay away from.

## Understanding radial spread

Radial spread, an artifact of the Stormscope, used to be a real problem with the early models. It required a fair amount of pilot experience and skill to interpret correctly. The Series II is much improved in this respect but radial spread does show up, generally in three forms.

The most common is a sprinkling of spurious discharge points (crosses) toward the center of the CRT from the main cluster of a strong storm. This phenomenon is quite obvious, and requires little interpretative skill.

The next most common is a loose pattern of individual discharge points off the nose of the aircraft at about the 200-mile circle. This indicates that either a strong thunderstorm is just beyond the 200-mile range or that electromagnetic discharges are arriving by atmospheric skip from a distant storm that's well beyond the instrument's range.

The least common form sometimes occurs when there is a strong storm at about the 50-mile range. Suddenly a thunderstorm cluster seems to pop up between you and it. This could be radial spread or it could be a new, and fast-growing, thunderstorm. If in VMC, looking out the window will tell you what's going on; if in IMC, treat it as real and, as soon as possible, get it off to the side of one of your 30-degree lines.

## Random discharges

Random discharge points, which are often confusing to those new to the Stormscope, are usually caused by atmospheric instability associated with cumulus clouds, or developing/dissipating thunderstorms. Use your CLEAR button regularly, and monitor the discharge points. Dissipating storms will disappear; developing cells will build; and cumulus clouds that are trying to make up their minds will come and go indecisively.

Some pilots believe that embedded thunderstorms are less serious than those that are not embedded. This type of thinking is a mistake. Embedded cells are more than strong enough to get you on the 11 o'clock news and should be treated accordingly.

Embedded storms do not seem to put out as much lightning as airmass or frontal storms; therefore even very small clusters or scatters of dots are important. My advice is to keep all of them outside the 30-degree lines when they are within 50 miles.

When VFR, on a hot hazy day when the lifted index is showing minus and the K-index is in the 20s to 30s, the Series II Stormscope (set to the 100- or 200-mile range in the 360-degree configuration) proves valuable for keeping up with the big picture. Some pilots prefer to use the 120-degree forward range for the big picture, for they are mainly interested in where they are going.

I feel somewhat differently. I like to know where my outs are if things begin to get too interesting, and, in my experience, outs are all too often behind or to the side of my course.

The Stormscope is not designed for storm penetration, it's designed for avoidance. However, winding through a line or group of cells is often necessary. Whether this can be done safely or not depends on how close together the cells are.

When penetrating lines or groups of cells, keep all clusters outside the 30-degree lines. If it begins to look as if this will not be possible, then it's time to put Plan B into effect. (You do have a Plan B, I hope.) My Plan B is usually to land and sit the storms out in comfort. I'm always monitoring my chart and loran for nearby airports. However, if matters got serious enough—being well used to off-airport landings from years in the Arctic—I wouldn't hesitate to use a country road and, if necessary, tie the plane to a farmer's fence.

## Notes on briefings

I noted earlier that I've never had the dubious pleasure of seeing a tornado on my Stormscope's CRT. That is because I plan carefully for my flights when thunderstorms are likely, and stay out of the dangerous areas. I am an avid fan of the radar summary chart (which also shows the severe-thunderstorm and tornado watch boxes), and make a point of avoiding the critical areas when a watch is current. I know that even with my Stormscope those areas are trouble and will be a problem.

If possible, I plan a different route. If that is not feasible, I scrub the flight until things improve. Most pilots interested in thunderstorms also become interested in the stability charts (lifted and K-index), and it takes very little experience with them to learn to predict the areas where trouble might arise later in the day or perhaps during the early evening. Loyal fans of the stability charts include Dennis Newton and Jerry Smith and I recommend the charts highly.

Since thunderstorm research is still in its infancy, new discoveries are being made daily. One of the more recent flashes of awareness was that thunderstorms develop not only as individual airmass storms or in lines, but that they also tend to congregate in large, roughly circular or elliptical patterns. These groups often have a diameter of several hundred miles and have a tendency to remain fairly stationary for extended periods. The NOAA has labeled this phenomenon the Mesoscale Convective Complex, or MCC for short. If your briefing indicates that there is MCC activity in the vicinity of your destination, give serious thought before launching. This phenomenon can last for many hours.

## Conclusion

It is my opinion that the Series II Stormscope is a safety device of such importance that when thunderstorms are likely and the trip is IFR (in a no-radar airplane), it's a go/no-go item. Even in hazy-VFR weather, it is a valuable adjunct to visual avoidance and well worth having. When visibility is 5 to 7 miles, trouble can come up fast at the cruising speed of even a small single like my Cessna 206, and forewarned is surely forearmed. If used for its intended purpose—avoidance, not penetration—a Stormscope will allow you to complete many flights safely that would otherwise not be possible.

*We've emphasized that ATC radars are not optimized to depict weather. Nevertheless, they do, and that information can be useful if a pilot knows what to ask for. It's important to realize that this information is limited and that ATC really can't provide as much information about the weather as many pilots believe. However, once you understand how ATC radar works and what it can do, you can make use of that limited information.*

*In this section Dave Gwinn, a recognized authority on airborne weather radar, talks about how to use ATC to help you steer clear of weather.*

## Weather Avoidance with Center Radar

Well, do they or don't they? One Center controller tells you "we don't paint weather." The next implies that they might but cautions "your radar is better than mine for that information." Then you overhear a controller giving both advice, specifics and vectors to another pilot who must own a bigger, better airplane than yours and thus is entitled to better services. One controller answered our DC-9 request with this: "They took all that capability out of our radars. We don't display any weather at all."

The confusion is understandable. Consider this: I recently conducted a radar seminar for a large business aircraft group. It was attended by seven Center controllers who, along with other FAA personnel, were invited as my guests.

At the conclusion of our Center radar discussion, one controller spoke for all seven: "I've never seen that directive (7110.76B, the one we'll discuss in a moment). None of us have had even *this* level of training in understanding our display."

Why, you might ask, is this so? The ATC system has been inundated with training and shy of staff since PATCO's day in the OK-Corral. Weather advisories are a "workload permitting" service so weather displays haven't been an ATC training priority.

But the information is there for the asking. Whether we like it our not, it's up to we pilots to inform ourselves about what's available and then ask for it.

## See weather? Of course

Make no mistake, Center radar doesn't paint weather as efficiently as airborne weather radar. But it does provide a usable weather return. It has limitations but it has value, too, if you understand the potential. The ARTCC weather display can often penetrate areas where airborne radar has expended its energy. It some cases, it might be the only weather-water-radar advice available, especially if you're flying one of the many GA aircraft with no radar at all. If you're in IMC, you can and should call for ARTCC assistance, since you're working with that controller anyway and because Center radar really can provide valuable input.

Understanding how the thing works is the first step. ARTCC radars are L-band, meaning they operate at 1000 mHz. These are the lowest frequency radars in the aviation field and for good reason. The lower the frequency, the longer the wavelength, the better the penetration over the great distances Center radars serve.

My voice is often described as bass. I'm told my voice is audible through classroom doors. That's low-frequency penetration. Conversely, with my hearing damaged by three decades of flying, a higher-pitched voice is difficult for me to discern. It doesn't penetrate.

Center's L-band radar tends to penetrate and ignore all weather. It reflects off of airplanes with that low-frequency "bass" wavelength. That's consistent with ATC's mission: See and separate aircraft from aircraft, not necessarily aircraft from weather.

## The Belly-Flop Principle

To the L-band wavelength, water droplets are about as much of an energy impediment as a gerbil is to a pit bull. Individual water droplets just don't exist to L-band radars. The water area has mass and resistance, not analytical droplet potential. However, L-band does receive *some* water information through a principle I call the belly-flop concept. (Don't repeat that to a radar engineer.)

Most kids do belly-flops into swimming pools. They hurt. Pain results from the water's flat surface boundary resisting your entry. In the same way, all radar energy encounters boundary resistance. A random and very ill-focused trickle is reflected back to the antenna and receiver. It's an absolutely insignificant return compared to an airborne radar display but ARTCC radars operate at five million watts or more.

Even a trickle of five megawatts is a lot of energy. It's not definitive but it's a crude return from which crude analysis can be made. You might say it senses only light to moderate resistance; anything greater is fuzzy.

It that's true (and it is) then we have a two-level radar display whose worst-case detection ability is moderate rainfall or better. In other words, it's capable of enough definition to tell light from moderate but moderate could really be anything up extreme level-6 activity.

## It has the capability

People who insist that ARTCC radar has no weather capability must be surprised when they learn that within the system is a digitized circuit called the Weather Fixed Map Unit (WFMU in ATC jargon). It receives and quantifies these rough returns and displays them to controllers by the selection of three weather keys: WX-1, WX-2 and WX-3.

The use of these keys was first defined in 1980 in a document entitled Narrowband Weather (Radar) Subsystem or 7110.76. Some quotes are worthy of note as we discuss the system. First, this: "The weather #1 and #2 keys will be selected in accord with weather and operational requirements. Both keys shall be selected when providing ATC radar inflight weather-avoidance assistance." Since no part of a controller's job relates solely to meteorology, "weather...requirements" must be stipulated by the pilot.

When the controller jabs WX-1, it triggers a precipitation summons from the WFMU to produce green slashes on the ARTCC display. These slashes represent that light boundary resistance return I explained in the previous section. The manual tells controllers that slashes represent light precipitation. That's correct and would correlate well with a pilot's level-1 (green) display, somewhere around .10 to .15 inches of rainfall per hour. If only the WX-1 key is used, the slashes will represent everything from light rain on up.

Airborne radars would present a green area as equating to 20 decibels (dBz) of returned energy. Anyone raising a teenager understands decibels as the singular reason you considered summoning Dr. Death from Michigan for a Mercy Retreat. Decibels, however, are simply a measure of power, including sound. The basic math is that decibels are nothing more than a logarithmic expression of a percentage, thus, a 40 decibel return is not twice as much energy as a 20 dBz return but 100 times as much. A higher decibel return represents a much higher rainfall rate.

This starts to come into play when the WX-2 key is engaged. Assuming there's enough moisture out there, the WX-2 produces little Hs on the controller's display. Engineering data tells us that Hs get born at about 28 to 30 decibels. To non-engineers, that's about .2 to .4 inches of rainfall per hour. It would correlate to level 2 or yellow on the pilot's airborne display.

Any professional pilot will tell you that level-2 rainfall should be avoided, if any options exist. It's noisy, you can't see and no one *invites* water ingestion into engines, piston or jet. And how yellow is yellow? Almost any sensible radar policy will call for avoiding convective level-3 (red) returns. There's a thin line of demarcation between the end of yellow and the beginning of red. In the upper 15 percent of yellow, you're approaching all the hazards of red, differing only in minor discomfort. So any level 2 might be "high yellow," and uncomfortably near red.

That's the extent of ARTCC's display so they have a level-1 and level-2 weather display and only that. However, anything could be buried and camouflaged within those Hs. It might be level 2 or it might be cumulo-granite. For that reason, the 7110.76 says this: "In the absence of other information, consider the worst-case scenario".

The worst case, of course, is level 6. That's certainly a conservative interpretation of what the Hs really represent. Could be, a herd of Hs covering an entire state is nothing but a harmless rain area, barely over level 2. But it could just as well be a level-6 mega-cell and you can bet that it doesn't get much worse than that.

I mentioned one other key, the WX-3. When the controller engages it, the display shows *both* slashes and Hs, assuming there's enough water out there to produce the appropriate return. You're usually interested in both so ask for the weather 3 key.

## Getting some help

As I said, ATC hasn't exactly made weather avoidance a priority. In most cases, you'll have to ask for assistance. I might say something like this: "Center, I'll bet that on the upper row of that block of keys to your left, the first three say 1, 2 and 3. I'll betcha if you pushed that 3 key and you talked to me about those Hs you might see, the Lord would bless you abundantly."

Okay, so maybe you wouldn't phrase it that way exactly but you get the idea. Keep it gentle. Convey your education and expectations. There's no need for conflict, argumentation or a position from which an ego-healthy controller cannot retreat. After all, *he's* got the keys and the information you want. And anyway, in the last ten years, only two controllers have been reluctant to supply me with safety information and I ask all the time.

If you've got no radar aboard, Center's assistance will be helpful. But you can also use ARTCC radar to supplement your onboard equipment. Caution is advised: Since ARTCC and airborne radar are apples and oranges, comparing the two is confusing. From the cockpit, we see level-2 water and while it's not inviting, it's not a threat, either. Then the weather-volunteering controller pops the weather key and sees a bunch of Hs. "I see you heading toward the heaviest part of the storm."

What storm? A pilot who lacks confidence in his radar capabilities might reason like this: "Now I'm not certain. This is a $50,000 radar and he has a $5-million installation. Radar is his job. Perhaps I don't know how to use mine as well as I thought."

But don't forget that the controller has no latitude in his interpretation ("in the absence of other information") and has to give you the worst possible case. However, your pirep might be the "other information" the controller needs. It's also confusing that the last three controllers told you "we don't paint weather," and now one is cautioning you based on his display. What the heck?

## Way out there

While ARTCC radar is quite penetrating, it's still distance-limited to about 125 nautical miles from the antenna site. Your position relative to the antenna might severely limit the information the controller can provide. That might be worth an inquiry before you challenge the controller's willingness to help you. In any case, the ARTCC radar may extend your view of the weather many miles beyond the range of your onboard equipment.

Two years ago, in rain and paralleling a squall line near Austin, our X-band airborne display indicated the end of the line in about 60 miles. We were suspicious of that. "Center, please use your weather-2 key and tell us how far south of our position you are displaying Hs?" His reply: "I'm showing Hs about 100 miles along your track. My range is depleted about there." That was useful information. It confirmed the attenuation which we suspected our airborne radar was suffering.

Again, using the radar techniques I teach in my seminars, it appeared to me that a break in a Minnesota squall line was attractive to entry. It was reasonably wide. Most important, we could tilt down and get good solid ground returns on the other side of the line. That indicated that a plentiful amount of radar energy remained beyond the line itself. (If you can't ground-paint through weather, don't ever *fly* through it.)

But one other piece of information was available for the decision: "Center, use your weather-2 key and I'll bet you're not showing any quantity of Hs ahead of our flight path." He wasn't. He was given what I expected him to see and he confirmed it. Otherwise, the controller's own random information might not have been useful to us. Had we asked, "What do you see?" it might have been a discourse on every area but the one we wanted.

By the way, if you're VFR and not working Center, get the appropriate frequency through FSS. When the sky gets dark and the rain shafts plentiful, there's safety and security in finding a path around and through those slashes and Hs, especially now that you know what it all means.

# Thunderstorm
# Tactics

---

There have been (and no doubt will be) many pilots who just can't seem to get it through their heads that the best thing to do about thunderstorms is stay away from them, period. Even pilots who always want to turn and run in the face of convective activity sometimes find themselves face-to-face with a thunderstorm.

In this section noted aviation author and contributing editor Richard Taylor passes on some hard-earned lessons about dealing with thunderstorms.

## Embedded Thunderstorm Tactics

Despite new ways of detecting thunderstorms, the hazards of an encounter with one are no different now than they ever have been. There are storm detection systems that show the location of electrical discharges; airborne radar points out precipitation areas; ATC radar can sometimes be helpful and we also have the human eyeball (perhaps the best indicator of all). Any pilot who ignores these indications and plows into a thunderstorm is in for the ride of his/her life...or worse.

It's difficult to imagine anyone flying into a known thunderstorm, and it's even more unlikely that you would put yourself in that circumstance, since we believe that our readers are more safety conscious than the average aviator. So it seems that a treatise with the avowed purpose of warning pilots away from thunderstorms is like preaching to the choir. But *au contraire:* there are meteorological traps out there just waiting for a stumbling pilot who would otherwise avoid them like the plague.

Most pilots who fly for a living in the thunderstorm-prone parts of the country have had the unhappy experience of getting into a thunderstorm or coming close enough to feel the effects. The energy expended by even the smallest storm is awesome. I know, you've heard that so often, your sensitivity has been dulled by repetition. But unless you have a burning desire to walk close to the edge, you don't want to challenge a thunderstorm in any airplane, *any* airplane.

There's no feeling of bravado, no psychological rush, or for that matter, no real satisfaction in winning a battle with a thunderstorm. I guarantee that you'll come away with the determination to never let it happen again. In a word, it's scary.

I've been there a few times in 38 years of flying and there is nothing short of a life-or-death situation that will get me to knowingly fly into a thunderstorm. Even then, I'd probably think of another way to get the job done. There's always another way; 38 years of flying has taught me that.

Many years ago (before I got smart), I was returning to Columbus, Ohio from Toledo, Ohio in an Aztec at 5000 feet in IMC. Thunderstorms were forecast that evening and I was listening closely to other pilots and the controllers as they advised each other about cells picked up by eyeball and on radar. Just before Toledo Departure handed me off to Center, he said, "For your information, the state police just reported that a tornado touched down near McComb, Ohio." I acknowledged that, then I realized that something else was near McComb, Ohio...my Aztec!

After a short pause, the controller asked, "Would you like to return to Toledo?"

I replied, "You might as well give me a clearance, I've already turned around and I'm headed that way." By that time, the clouds around me had turned an ugly yellow-brown and I wanted out of there...pronto. Stupid to be there? Yes. Smart to get out ASAP? Yes.

## The heart of the problem

Thunderstorms are bad enough when you have the good fortune to see what you're flying into, but the embedded variety are the worst of all. There's little opportunity to get yourself and the airplane prepared for the encounter. The turbulence/rain/lightning/hail is upon you so fast that the war may be over the instant the battle begins.

A significant storm system is often surrounded by thick layers of cloud that very effectively obscure the real danger. When there's a huge amount of energy stirring up a relatively small volume of airspace, some of the visible moisture (clouds) is bound to spread out and form visual barriers.

You might get away with only a bumpy ride by remaining well away from the storm as you fly in the cloud shield alongside the main body of the storm. But what if your heading takes you right to the heart of the bloody thing? When you can't see where you're going, it's a crap shoot and the odds are definitely not in your favor. Storms move, winds change, at two or three miles a minute, and you could be in serious trouble in short order.

Avoidance is the only sure technique to ensure your survival and there are several ways to go about it. First, never fly in clouds when there are thunderstorms in the forecast. That severely limits the utility of your airplane, but when you consider the alternative, utility slips into second place.

You could compromise and decide to never share a cloud system with embedded thunderstorms unless you have storm detection gear on board. That's one step better than not seeing at all, but consider that the manufacturers of radar and other electronics are not willing to say that their products should be used to pick your way through a storm system. This equipment is for avoidance, period.

Suppose you decide to let electrons do the looking for you and you head down an avenue that seems clear of nastiness. But when you turn the next corner to avoid a cell, there's an even bigger one. Now there's nothing but retreat and the storms can close in around you in the blink of an eye. Radar and its kin have definite limitations. Respect them.

There are two more solutions better suited to pilots of light aircraft. First, fly in clear air where you can pick out the storms visually and avoid them absolutely. Second, fly underneath and circumnavigate the rain shafts, thereby avoiding the hazards of the storm.

The clear air solution is a good one, but doesn't always work. Let's change that to "seldom works." Most light aircraft don't have the power and performance to remain in clear air close to thunderstorms. This technique is okay for avoiding isolated cells, but when a line of storms lies across your intended route, you can count on a climb to at least 15,000 feet to clear those big piles of clouds. You can also count on the storms building behind you, so that when the ones in front force a turn, you'll be circling in a constantly narrowing canyon of clouds with nowhere to go. This is a most uncomfortable place to be and it will get worse.

"So high you can't get over it, so low you can't get under it," is a song that speaks volumes about thunderstorms, especially when the song is sung by the pilot of a light airplane. Heading for the deck and staying out of the rain shafts is acceptable sometimes, but not when the accompanying cloud deck is so low that obstruction clearance is compromised nor when storm-induced turbulence is present in clear air.

Have you ever stood in the path of a storm and experienced the rush of wind that usually arrives ahead of the rain? That's the outflow (sometimes a downburst) inevitable when volumes of descending cold air meet the ground and fan out in all directions. Do you really want to put your airplane in the path of all that wind?

In IFR operations, there's another major limitation to beating the storm by flying low. That's the problem you'll have continuing safely on an instrument clearance. Controllers are charged with keeping airplanes away from each other, and on frequent occasion when dealing with a low-level storm avoider, they are forced to change your routing to ensure separation. Of course, you can always refuse a vector or routing that will put you too close to a storm for comfort, but you can't expect to fly the rest of the way home like that. Confrontations with controllers are usually as productive as confrontations elsewhere.

## What do you paint up ahead?

Finally, every instrument pilot needs to have a crystal-clear understanding that ATC radar is not a weather-avoidance tool. There was a time when controllers could see precipitation on their displays and some of them did a good job of helping pilots avoid the biggies. But today's radar is designed for one purpose, traffic separation.

The controllers see only two levels of precipitation. If you associate precipitation echoes with turbulence, the two levels are, 'Maybe I can get through there with only a few bumps,' and 'Maybe the wings will be torn off,' which isn't an acceptable solution. Be very mindful that controllers can tell you only whether they see areas of precipitation or that they don't see any. Bottom line: Don't rely on ATC radar for thunderstorm information.

## An embedded dilemma?

The pilots who have come to grief from unsuccessful bouts with embedded thunderstorms decided that getting there was more important than getting there in one piece. Some of them might have complained that a controller didn't tell them about the storms hidden in the clouds. Some might have tried to climb over the weather and came up short because the airplane wouldn't climb any more. And some might have ignored forecasts or weather reports indicating the presence of thunderbumpers in a larger cloud system.

No matter, because they fought the weather and lost. If you don't have reliable storm detection equipment and know how to use and interpret it, or if you don't have an airplane that can climb well up into the teens and twenties (with oxygen), you're better off to avoid an embedded thunderstorm situation completely.

You don't have to challenge thunderstorms to become a respected pilot. You should have the common sense and respect for the safety of yourself and your passengers that leads you to avoid thunderstorms at all costs, especially when you can't see where you're going.

*Unfortunately, somtimes you just can't avoid that cell. Strange, violent things happen inside thunderstorms, and if you're to escape an encounter with one you need to know what to expect.*

*CFII John W. Conrad here gives some further advice on avoiding thunderstorms, and what to do if you find yourself caught in one.*

## Thunderstorm Encounters

I've had the misfortune of having flown into three fully-developed thunderstorms in the last 20 years. Each close encounter of the thunderstorm kind was in an airplane not equipped with either radar or Stormscope. That's the bad news. The good news is I survived and have managed to avoid flying into thunderstorms ever since.

Canceling your flight whenever thunderstorms are forecast means you won't do much flying in the warmer months. Whenever there's moist, unstable air, there's a potential for thunderstorm activity. Under these circumstances, the National Weather Service issues a forecast for thunderstorms along with a sigmet and perhaps a severe weather warning.

The first question following a forecast of thunderstorm activity should be, What does the radar summary chart look like? Unlike most of what we get in a standard weather briefing, the radar summary tells the trained observer exactly where the thunderstorms are and their general level of intensity.

By comparing several of these charts, it's possible to tell how fast the thunderstorms are building and their direction of movement. So even though a gloom-and-doom forecast might predict thunderstorm activity in the general area, it's possible the actual thunderstorms are far removed from your planned route. Or it might be possible to select an alternate route that skirts the thunderstorm activity altogether.

The best strategy for dealing with thunderstorms in flight is to maintain VFR and keep them in sight. When VFR below the clouds, the columns of rain and dust being kicked-up on the ground give a clear indication of the worst parts.

If you have a turbocharged engine or two, you might be able to get on top of the clouds and steer around the buildups. I don't recommend this in a normally-aspirated airplane. Any thunderstorm worth mentioning will top-out way above the service ceiling of a normally-aspirated airplane. Yet if the thunderstorms are widely spaced it might be possible to remain VFR on top, below the service ceiling of the airplane, and fly completely around the buildups.

Here's where pireps are handy. The reports and forecasts of the tops reflect the highest thing around. I've made many flights where the tops were reported in excess of 30,000 feet, but the flight was easily completed below 10,000 feet by steering around the widely-scattered tops.

## Report early and often

Anyone successfully completing a flight in difficult weather who doesn't file a pilot report is simply not house-broken. Pireps are the best information a person on the ground can get. To complete a difficult flight and then not share the information with the rest of the world should be a capital crime.

If you're on an IFR flight plan, both you and the controller will be involved in trying to balance actual weather conditions, traffic, rules and regulations and aircraft performance in order to avoid the thunderstorms and complete the flight.

A pilot in IMC cannot see thunderstorms embedded in the clouds. So if there is a monster ahead on the airway, you could roar right into it, fat dumb and happy. Even without storm detection equipment, there's still some information available.

Sometimes, the best information comes from airplanes ahead of you on the airway. Ask the controller who is up there and how they're doing. You can even talk to them directly. For example, if you're 10 miles behind a Cessna 172 and the pilot reports a good ride, there's a good chance you'll get the same. But there's no guarantee. Thunderstorms are seldom stationary. It's entirely possible for one to slide in front of you after the last airplane passed .

Flight Watch and flight service can often provide real-time radar weather analysis and pireps to help avoid thunderstorms and other areas of severe weather. This should be done before departure, but is also useful en route in making decisions. Although ATC radar is primarily for the control of traffic, many times controllers can, when requested, offer suggested headings and/or routes to avoid severe weather based on their radar displays.

## Survival Techniques

If you fly in IMC with embedded thunderstorms, sooner or later you'll fly into one. You might get lucky (like I did) and fly for a long time before you bump into one. After your first encounter, though, you'll never want to do it again. Nevertheless, an encounter with a thunderstorm need not be fatal, but it requires a tremendous amount of technique and self-control.

A review of in-flight break-ups following a thunderstorm encounter shows the airplane was actually destroyed by the pilot's loss of control. Excess airspeed seems to be the key factor in many of these accidents. The evidence indicates many aircraft were going too fast when they broke up. So in a violently turbulent situation, it's most important to keep airspeed under control.

Unfortunately, in a thunderstorm, the airspeed indicator is virtually useless for controlling airspeed. The rapid wind shears and pressure changes make the instrument unreliable. The turbulence can be so violent your eyes cannot track the instruments. In severe turbulence, the instrument panel looks like a blur. Yet you can still control airspeed by keeping the wings level and trimming for a slow controllable speed.

## Trim effects

The trim on most airplanes establishes a relationship of aerodynamic balance between the wing, which is producing up lift, and the tail which is producing down lift. In most airplanes exhibiting positive dynamic stability, if the airspeed increases the tail will automatically add additional pitch forces and try to raise the nose to slow down. Conversely, if the airspeed gets slow, the tail will lose some down lift and the nose will drop allowing the airspeed to build.

In fast airplanes, this dynamic stability is minimal at cruise speed. As the airplane is slowed to near maneuvering or approach speed, the dynamic stability usually increases. Furthermore, we know the forces on an airplane increase dramatically with speed. You should first slow down when flying a high-performance aircraft and encountering severe turbulence or a thunderstorm.

Because the body of knowledge about successful thunderstorm penetrations is limited, there's no FAA-approved procedure other than the admonition, "Don't do it." As pilot in command, you must make your own decisions.

Turbulence penetration is a subject that requires careful review of your pilot's operating handbook. Not all aircraft have the same procedure. However, engineering and flight test data almost always specify that severe turbulence penetration must first consider maneuvering speed and gross weight. Be prepared with knowledge of the specific aircraft you're flying before entering areas of possible severe turbulence.

## Small control inputs

While doing all this, I concentrate on keeping the wings level and the nose on the horizon by using very small control deflections. In a thunderstorm, you won't be able to see the attitude indicator very often. As I mentioned earlier, in severe turbulence your head and the airplane will be bouncing around so much your eyes won't be able to track the instruments.

You'll have to wait for a calm moment to the desired correction. What you're looking for is an average wings-level attitude. There will also be times following lightning flashes when you won't be able to see the instruments. Following the flash you'll see nothing but dozens of brightly glowing sugar crisps swimming around before your eyes.

It's important not to roll the airplane in either direction when you can't see the instruments. Just wait to make a correction until you have some control.

## Don't worry about altitude

During all this, you'll have no control over the altitude. Under normal circumstances the best climb or descent you could get would be 1500 fpm. The up and down drafts in a thunderstorm can be 10 times that. Likewise, don't worry about the heading. Keep the wings level and you'll stay as close to your last heading as possible.

Keep the nose on the horizon and the wings level. Whatever you do, don't turn around. You'll only prolong the agony and any bank will dramatically increase structural loading.

A thunderstorm encounter can be survived, but the best course of action is avoid them altogether. In order to do that, you must be able to remain VFR either below the overcast, between layers or on top.

## Avoid at all costs

Tell ATC if you get to the point where you can't maintain VFR, then reverse course and remain in the clear. Otherwise, if you continue flying in IMC with embedded thunderstorms, you'll eventually have an experience similar to mine. And it's one experience I recommend avoiding.

# Ice
# Avoidance

B*efore you launch into winter IFR, there are several things you must consider regardless of whether your aircraft has the capability to deal with ice.* *There are those who intentionally fly into icing knowing they aren't properly equipped and others who believe that because their aircraft has boots and hot props, they can handle whatever they encounter. Both these attitudes are dangerous and can lead to a serious confrontation with mother nature, who seldom loses.*

## Ice Briefing

Whether you use DUAT or an FSS for your briefings, you must have the latest information on icing conditions. There are several places to look for this information.

Until recently, the National Weather Service (NWS) predicted icing conditions in the synopsis section of the area forecast. Now, NWS issues airmets that indicate what you should expect in your area. These airmets can be called up on DUAT by using the identifier WA.

Airmets are intended to be in-flight advisories, but are just as effective before you leave the ground. They provide alerts for weather hazardous to light aircraft, including known or forecast moderate icing. Sigmets (WS) are issued for weather conditions hazardous to all aircraft and include the expectation of severe icing.

A lot can be learned from pilot reports. For example, when the pilot of a Boeing 727 reports severe icing during descent below 7000 feet, these are conditions you don't want to encounter in a Cessna 172.

The airline pilot made that report because the ice build-up was more than his de-icing equipment could handle. Usually large jet aircraft climb and descend through the clouds so rapidly that they aren't greatly affected. So when you see a report from a large aircraft reporting moderate or severe icing, you know conditions are at the extreme for a light aircraft.

## Other sources

After reviewing the pireps and airmets, if you're still unsure of the conditions, you could call the local approach control or tower. Sometimes pilots report icing to ATC, but these reports never get to an FSS or DUAT. Controllers use these reports to warn other aircraft on the frequency.

Another source of conditions aloft are from pilots who have just landed. While it isn't information from an approved source, if a corporate pilot tells you about moderate icing between 2000 and 6000 feet and you're planning to cruise at 5000 feet in a light single, you'd better wait for another day.

## Check winds aloft

Reviewing the winds aloft forecasts indicates the temperatures you should expect at the lower, ice-producing altitudes. We were flying a Beech Baron from Columbus, Ohio to Atlantic City, New Jersey and picked up ice from shortly after takeoff until passing 8500 feet where we topped the cloud layer. We knew the tops were between 8000 and 9000 feet from pireps we had seen on DUAT and believed the aircraft's de-icing equipment would be sufficient to get us on top. It was.

We also knew from the winds aloft forecast that as we proceeded eastbound the temperatures would rise from the surface through our cruising altitude, so getting down would be no problem. Approaching the Philadelphia area, we knew ATC would start our descent a long distance from my destination. If the temperatures hadn't been as warm as forecast, we wouldn't have attempted that flight, since we would have been stuck at icing altitudes for too long.

## Known icing

If you're flying a single or twin that lacks de-ice equipment, be aware the FAA considers known icing to exist any time there's a forecast of any ice (even if it's light) or if there are any reports of ice in the clouds. An airplane that isn't certificated to fly in known icing isn't legal to fly in the clouds under those conditions.

I recently asked an FAA inspector about an aircraft without de-icing gear climbing through a thin cloud layer to get on top when icing conditions are forecast. He said it's illegal, but if no incident, accident or emergency occurs you probably won't get caught.

But is it prudent to go out in icing conditions your airplane isn't certificated to fly in? It's often impossible to predict what ATC will do with your flight. You could wind up in the clouds for considerably longer than you had planned, picking up ice the whole time. If you declare an emergency to get out of the icing conditions, an investigation of the incident will disclose you didn't have the required gear, which could lead to a violation.

## Even if you're equipped

Accumulating ice on an airframe leads to two problems. First, the ice adds weight and will slow you down. Second, ice changes the shape of the wing and other aerodynamic surfaces and spoils lift. An airplane with full de-icing gear is not immune from these two problems and can get into serious trouble if a pilot stays in icing conditions too long.

An airplane certificated for known icing has a combination of anti-icing and de-icing equipment. The anti-icing gear must be turned on before entering the clouds when icing is forecast. Generally a heated windshield, stall vent, fuel vent, pitot tube and electric or alcohol propeller systems fall under this category. The de-icing boots found on the wings and tail surfaces are exercised after ice builds to between a quarter and half inch. The misuse of these systems can lead to problems.

For example, on some airplanes, turning the windscreen heat on after ice has collected on it can lead to a deformed windscreen if the heat melts the inner layer of ice but leaves the outer layer in place. It doesn't take long for the water next to the windscreen to boil and overheat the panel.

When using de-ice boots, exercising them too early will cause the ice to take the shape of the extended boot. After that, as ice continues to gather, it will form in that shape making the boots worthless.

An airplane with a known icing package can't always remain in icing conditions for an entire flight. Remember, there are surfaces, like the cowlings, tip tanks, portions of wings that don't have boots, the copilot's windscreen if it isn't heated and other areas where ice accumulates and cannot be shed. This ice adds weight to the aircraft and slows it down considerably.

The longer the aircraft remains in the ice, the slower it will get and its lift producing capabilities will be less efficient. With the added weight comes a higher stall speed and at some point the two must meet.

Older aircraft with an alcohol anti-ice system for the windshield, props or both require careful monitoring to ensure those surfaces stay clear of ice. The alcohol must be turned on before entering icing conditions to be effective. The size of the reservoirs in these systems are usually not conducive to remaining in the ice for very long.

## Don't delay

Regardless of whether your aircraft has de-ice gear, when encountering ice, start looking for a way out. Ask the controller about the cloud tops or layers (if known). If they're within reach of your aircraft, climb. Unless you intend to land, don't descend unless you're sure there's warmer air or reports of no ice below you.

Most controllers will help by asking other aircraft in the area about conditions. If you descend to a lower altitude and the ice accumulation continues, you'll have less altitude to play with in the event the situation gets serious.

Sometimes warmer air can be found at higher altitudes. Temperature inversions are common in the middle of weather systems. But finding one and shedding the ice you've accumulated might only be a temporary solution. If you run out of the inversion and back into colder air, you'll be back in icing conditions.

## Icing conditions

From -5 C to -20 C, the moisture in a cloud remains as super-cooled water droplets. When an airplane passes through the cloud these water droplets adhere to the airframe as ice. Normally, below -20 C these droplets tend to solidify and are unable to stick to the aircraft. When looking for a way out of icing, climbing to a higher, colder altitude might be an alternative.

Normally aspirated aircraft don't have the power to climb out of the lower icing altitudes. A turbocharged or turbine aircraft can normally get into the 'teens or higher, where the air might be cold enough to keep ice from accumulating.

## Forecast, but not there

Sometimes, when icing is forecast, there isn't any. There are several reasons why this might occur and you should think carefully and do your homework before launching when conditions say ice will be there and pireps say it isn't.

An icing forecast is issued when information suggests the conditions, such as temperature, cloud cover, moisture content, etc., exist. Also, these forecasts generally cover a large area and it's possible one part might experience the actual conditions and another might not.

Another possibility is that a system with ice-producing clouds might be moving faster or slower than earlier forecasts suggested. If it's moving slower, you could be fooled into thinking you can handle what is out there and launch, then find the very conditions you thought weren't there are just a few miles down the airway.

Another possibility to explore is getting around the icing conditions altogether. It might be possible to take a different route, undoubtedly longer than you planned, and fly around the system generating the icing problems. Whether you're IFR or VFR, this is the only real alternative for an aircraft that lacks de-icing gear, other than staying on the ground.

Carefully review the current surface chart to determine how wide an area the system you're watching covers. Should you attempt to fly around it or would it be more reasonable to sit and wait for it to pass? In the winter most systems move rapidly, and if the route around the weather would require more flight time than you're willing to commit, wait out the weather or cancel the trip.

## Takeoff accidents

Once a DC-9-10 crashed after takeoff due to what investigators determined was icing on the wings that accumulated during descent on the previous leg. The National Transportation Safety Board concluded the amount of ice that brought the airplane down might have been so little that the pilots probably didn't see it if they inspected the wing from the cabin. The crew didn't get out of the aircraft and look it over during the brief stop.

Other publicized takeoff accidents involving airframe icing alert us to be certain there's no ice, snow or frost adhering to the airplane before we roll. Yes, it's tough to scrape ice and frost from an airplane. It must be done, though, or else the airplane should be put in a warm hangar and de-iced. Another alternative is to spray the aircraft with a heated glycol/water mixture. This is what the airlines use to de-ice their airplanes before takeoff.

## Be alert regardless

We all know the weather service isn't one hundred percent accurate with their forecasting and we can't expect them to be. Therefore we must be alert for icing anytime we fly in the clouds when the temperatures are forecast to be in the icing range. Anti-ice or de-ice equipment isn't a sure cure for the icing problem, only a means of staying aloft until a way out of it can be found.

# • Section Three •

# Weather Hazards

# Weather
# Generators

Regardless of the season, the same forces are at work making the weather: the effects of solar heating, evaporation, collision of air masses and interaction of areas of differing pressure.

In this first chapter on specific weather phenomena, we'll take a look at the two most overt sources of weather: high and low pressure systems and fronts. The later chapters in this section will cover in detail some of the specific phenomena that result from the interaction of these weather generators.

## Highs and Lows

It's 6:45 in the morning. Rolling out of bed, you snap on the T.V. and hear the weather man say something about a high pressure system building over the area.

A fat red H appears on the screen, planting itself over your state. Oh boy, you think, nice flying weather for a few days. You'd better think again.

Blindly following the old forecasting rule of high pressure equals good weather, low pressure equals bad weather, exhibits poor judgment and can be an invitation to disaster.

Depending on the season, seemingly benign high pressure systems can exhibit sharp teeth in the form of violent air-mass thunderstorms. Low pressure systems, on the other hand, have been known to produce moderate weather, with acceptable visibility.

To understand why high and low pressure systems exhibit disagreeable characteristics, we need to understand what makes them tick. The first step is to review the mechanisms of their formation—global temperature and air circulation patterns.

## Temperature and circulation

When air over a large surface area is heated, the air becomes less dense and rises. When a surface area is cooled, the air over it becomes more dense and sinks. The air continues to rise and descend, creating a circulation pattern known as convection.

These differences in air temperature create differences in atmospheric pressure. Areas of cool temperatures, where the air descends and spreads out on the surface, produce high pressure. Areas of warm temperatures, where the air rises, create low pressure. On a global scale, the warmer areas, such as the tropics, tend to produce low surface pressure, and cool areas, such as the poles, create high pressure.

These global pressure differences produce and drive wind through the pressure gradient force. This force tries to push the air perpendicular to the isobars (lines connecting areas of equal pressure) and move it from high to low pressure. The stronger the pressure gradient, the stronger the resulting wind. When checking a pressure analysis chart, you can tell the strength of the winds by the isobar spacing, narrow spacing means strong winds, wide spacing means light winds.

If the earth did not rotate, the wind would blow perpendicular to the isobars, moving from the equator to the poles and back again. However, since the earth does rotate, the Coriolis force created by the spin deflects the wind at almost a 90 degree angle as soon as it begins to move, blowing it parallel to the isobars. (This is particularly noticeable on the upper air charts. Winds nearer the surface are reduced in part due to friction and blow at a slight angle across the isobars toward lower pressure.) The Coriolis force deflection is to the right in the Northern Hemisphere and to the left in the Southern Hemisphere. In the Northern Hemisphere, wind from the equator, which wants to blow directly north, instead moves to the right and blows to the northeast. Wind from the poles, trying to reach the south, blows from the east. Both of these large scale movements of air meet, overturn and blow westerly in the mid latitudes (30 degrees to 60 degrees). The air piles up, and, as it presses downward, creates a band of semi-permanent high pressure systems. This blockage disrupts air movement in the mid latitudes and sets the stage for the endless creation and progression of storms that move from west to east as cold and warm air masses clash.

Seasonal climate changes, which cause more localized surface heating and cooling, also play a part in generating pressure systems. The summertime heating of the North American continent produces low pressure, while the cooler Atlantic Ocean produces high pressure. This scenario is reversed in the winter months.

The high and low pressure systems that spawn in the turbulent mid latitudes have distinctive characteristics, ones that we must deal with every time we fly. They march across the continent, wave upon wave, creating an endless variety of weather to match. (In fact, if you could see a constant pressure analysis chart from the side, the continuous passage of highs and lows across the country would look very similar to the swell of the ocean's surface.)

## Three types of highs

High pressure systems, also called anticyclones, are zones of stable, dense air. As the air descends and pushes outward from the center, it is deflected to the right. Hence, the clockwise flow of air around a high. There are three types of anticyclones: subtropical highs, polar continental highs and highs that form between low pressure systems, often in the form of ridges.

Subtropical highs are usually found along the 30 degree latitude line in each hemisphere. They are huge, deep systems that are somewhat elliptical in shape and semi-permanent in nature.

One example of a semi-permanent subtropical high pressure system is the Bermuda High. In the summer, it positions itself off the southeast coast of the United States and pumps warm, moist air northward. This creates hot, humid days filled with violent storms, morning fog, and thick haze layers across the mid-section of the country and along the East Coast. The jet stream often blocks its movement northward, so it remains in a semi-stationary state until a strong storm, usually originating out of the northwest, knocks it out of the way.

Polar continental highs form over the northern continents in the winter. These highs, made of very cold air (-30 C, on average), are much smaller than the subtropical highs, generally one to two miles deep and a few hundred miles across. They move rather swiftly across the North American continent.

Ridges are elongated highs that form between low pressure systems. A contour analysis chart, which shows the contours of height of a constant pressure surface, displays the location of ridges. The rising atmospheric pressure within the high pushes the pressure surface upward into a ridge shape, with the highest pressure marking the area of maximum anticyclonic curvature (curvature of isobars to the right).

## Two types of lows

Low pressure systems, or cyclones, are zones of unstable, less dense air. The air rises and blows inward to the center, is deflected and blows counterclockwise in the Northern Hemisphere. There are two types of lows: tropical and extratropical.

Tropical lows, also known as hurricanes, form over the warm waters of the Atlantic and Pacific Oceans near the equator. In the Atlantic, tropical lows often form off the coast of Africa and move westward as they grow into hurricanes. They follow the easterly trade winds until reaching the Caribbean, where they turn northward and occasionally make landfall along the south/southeast coast of the United States or the east coast of Mexico. Many of these hurricanes spin off into the North Atlantic, never touching land and dissipate around 40 degrees north latitude.

The pressure differences within a hurricane are extreme, with the pressure dropping to as low as 960 millibars (28.35 in) as the storm passes. The distinctive cumulus cloud spirals of a typical hurricane can extend outward to 900 miles. Embedded thunderstorms, intense precipitation and high winds are found within the spiral arms, as air is forced rapidly aloft. The opposite is true within the tiny eye (which is only a few miles in diameter), with winds and precipitation dropping to zero as the air sinks downward.

Extratropical cyclones are less intense storms that last longer and are spread out over a larger area than hurricanes, affecting weather over a greater distance and for a longer period of time. In the Northern Hemisphere, they form around 50 degrees north latitude in the winter and 60 degrees north latitude in the summer, typically forming over one spot in the North Pacific (often called the Aleutian Low for statistical purposes) and the North Atlantic (called the Icelandic Low) before moving on.

An extratropical low is a few thousand miles wide and as deep as the troposphere, which extends to approximately 30,000 feet. In the United States, these lows move across the country with regularity, and are almost always accompanied by fronts and the ensuing bad weather. As the low matures, the fronts proceed through various stages until reaching occlusion, after which the low dissipates.

Troughs are elongated areas of low pressure, similar to ridges, with the lowest pressure found along a line that marks the maximum cyclonic curvature, or curvature of isobars to the left. Since these are typically upper air phenomena, they will not show up on a surface analysis chart; however, they can seriously affect weather at the surface, making a review of the upper level pressure analysis chart almost mandatory.

## Cold and thermal lows

Two other types of low pressure systems, which are subcategories of the extratropical lows, can exist. Known as cold lows and thermal lows, they are complete opposites in terms of characteristics.

A cold low is a cold, very intense low pressure system that is almost vertical in structure. (Both highs and lows lean somewhat from the surface into the upper atmosphere. This slope, the angle of which can vary from shallow to steep, causes the upper winds to blow across any associated surface systems. Surface systems are steered by the upper wind currents in the direction of the current flow.)

Because the slope in a cold low is extremely steep, the upper winds tend to go around a surface low, thereby slowing its movement. As many of us know, a slow-moving low can bring extensive low-cloudiness, heavy precipitation and strong winds that can last for several days.

A thermal low forms when surface heating generates a low-level low over an area with little moisture, such as a desert. The warm air rises, but no clouds form. This type of low is weak, with a shallow slope and a clear lack of cyclonic circulation. It usually produces good flying weather, except for some turbulence.

Remember that pressure systems produce wind, and wind moves the pressure systems. If you could stand along an isobar line, with lower pressure to your left, the wind will be blowing in the direction you are facing.

Upper winds steer the course for surface highs and lows, with the winds always crossing the isobars parallel to the contour in the upper altitudes toward low pressure. Surface winds at lower altitudes cross the isobars at an angle toward the lower pressure.

Highs and ridges are areas where the air is descending or sinking, making it difficult for clouds to form. However, since sinking air is dense and stable, it puts a cap on convective activity of all kinds and can lead to air stagnation after a period of days. This cap traps moisture and pollution, causing a drop in visibility. In addition, low stratus and fog can form in stagnant air. As the high matures and moves, the air can become unstable, allowing air-mass thunderstorms to form. Generally, upper highs and ridges will produce good flying weather—clear skies and good visibility.

Lows and troughs, on the other hand, are areas of ascending air and produce bad weather. Keep in mind that the upper air lows and troughs can cause considerable cloudiness and precipitation to develop at the surface ahead of them, irrespective of the surface weather.

Pilots who make uninformed assumptions about weather can have short-lived careers. So don't assume, check the weather thoroughly before you go and you'll be less likely caught in the teeth of a hungry high.

*The second major feature of weather patterns are the boundaries between differing air masses: fronts.*

*Frontal boundaries are areas of change, and thus are usually where the most weather activity is located. For a VFR pilot, fronts are things to be avoided. For an instrument pilot, however, fronts and the phenomena associated with them should be studied closely.*

## Frontal Systems

The prerecorded voice of the briefer drones out the recorded forecast: A warm front extending from southwestern Virginia through southern Arkansas will move slowly northward. Along the route until 0500 Zulu, three thousand scattered to broken, ceilings seven to ten thousand overcast, areas with ceilings one to two thousand overcast, visibility below three miles in light rain and fog. After 0500 Zulu, one to two thousand overcast with visibility three to five miles in fog, areas with ceilings below one thousand feet and visibility below three miles in light rain and fog. Flight precautions advised for thunderstorm activity, IFR conditions, icing, turbulence and mountain obscuration. This is not what you want to hear the day of your flight.

Frontal systems can cause considerable grief for the unsuspecting pilot. Knowing what to expect when crossing a front can mean the difference between an uneventful flight and one filled with uncertainty and tension.

## Air masses collide

Fronts result from the clash of two mighty titans—warm and cold air masses. You may recall from basic meteorology that an air mass is a large, continent-sized body of air relatively uniform in temperature and moisture content. When this air mass remains over a particular area of the earth's surface for a period of time, it acquires the properties of that area. Examples of these surface areas (called source areas) are deserts, tropical and polar oceans, and the snow-covered polar ice caps. A typical air mass over the North Pole is cold and dry, while one over the Gulf of Mexico is warm and moist.

Global weather propels these bodies of air at each other. The air masses shift position and pick up the properties of the areas over which they move. Air masses can be modified in several ways. If cold air moves over a warm surface, it is heated from below, thereby increasing instability and the possibility of precipitation.

Conversely, warm air moving over a cool surface is cooled from below, thereby increasing stability. When this air is cooled to its dew point, fog and/or stratus clouds form. Water vapor also modifies air masses. Evaporation from precipitation and water surfaces add vapor to the atmosphere. If the water is warmer than the air, fog and stratus develop. Water vapor is removed by precipitation.

When the air masses jockey for position, a zone of transition develops along the area of contact. This area of contact (or collision, depending on how you look at it) are known as frontal zones, or fronts for short.

Driven by the flow of the upper winds and jet streams, fronts move at different speeds (sometimes stopping to become stationary), reverse direction and even change character altogether. Some fronts produce considerable convective activity and precipitation, while other are dry and cloud-free, with only a wind shift to indicate passage, all depending on the type of air mass involved.

In most cases, you'll notice more than a wind shift when crossing a front. Temperature, dew point, wind direction and speed, and atmospheric pressure change markedly as you fly from one air mass to another.

As an instrument pilot, you will encounter the various fronts—warm, cold, occluded, stationary, and/or dew point—on a year-round basis. Each front has unique characteristics which vary according to the stability of the air masses and the seasons.

## Warm fronts

A warm front is the edge of an advancing warm air mass. The retreating cold air mass, which is denser than the warm air trying to replace it, remains close to the ground, making it difficult to push out of the way. The warm air is forced to move up and over the cold air, and replacement turns into a slow process taking as much as several days before frontal passage is complete. The frontal slope that results is long and gradual, spreading clouds and precipitation several hundred miles in advance of the front's surface position.

As mentioned previously, the clouds that form along a front vary depending on stability. If the warm air is stable, stratiform clouds exist. Layers of stratus descend lower and lower as the front advances and produce steady precipitation in the form of light rain and drizzle. The visibility deteriorates as smoke, haze and smog particles are trapped under the retreating cold air. Fog also forms. Little or no turbulence is present and the surface wind is light to moderate.

If the air is unstable, the warm front is likely to be studded with embedded thunderstorms, which results in sporadic heavy downpours and gusty winds in addition to the steady precipitation.

In the winter, warm front precipitation exists in the form of freezing rain and drizzle. This is the result of droplets falling from the wedge of warm air, where the temperature is above freezing, into the cold air underneath, where the temperature is below freezing. The droplets are supercooled through this process and freeze on contact. Snow falls when the temperature in the warm air is below freezing. Winter stratus clouds also contain rime ice due to the small droplet size.

Winter warm fronts can be particularly hazardous in the eastern U.S. due to the warm, humid air in the Gulf of Mexico and the southern Atlantic Ocean.

## Cold fronts

The edge of an advancing cold air mass, a cold front overtakes and replaces the retreating warm air in an abrupt fashion. The warm air is less dense and is easily thrown upward ahead of the cold air, creating considerable convective activity.

Violent squall lines can march ahead of fast moving cold fronts, clipping along at speeds of 20 to 50 knots. (Frontal passage usually occurs in a few hours.) Cumulonimbus tops can reach 50,000 feet or greater. The frontal slope is narrow due to the speed of movement, so heavy rain showers (snow showers in the winter) and gusty surface winds can occur from 20 to 300 miles in advance of the front.

In the winter, you can expect clear ice due to the heavy moisture content of the clouds and large droplet size. Also keep in mind the possibility of freezing rain. Moderate to severe turbulence and low-level wind shear exists with surface winds gusting to 50 knots.

Cold fronts vary in characteristics. Some are slow moving (less than 20 knots), while others are produced and backed by a shallow air mass, which creates a gradual frontal slope. With a gentle slope, you can expect the same weather found along a warm front (although the weather itself is far from gentle).

Other cold fronts are weak, meaning the properties of the air masses on either side of it are virtually indistinguishable. In this case, frontal passage is little more than the formation of a few broken or scattered layers of clouds and/or a change in surface wind direction.

The movement of a weak cold front is different from the normal north/south alignment and eastward movement of most fronts that sweep across the country. A weak cold front is usually aligned from west to east and moves slowly to the south. It sometimes becomes stationary and may advance northward again as a warm front. In a process called frontolysis, the weak cold front can also dissipate.

A cold front can also be transformed into an occluded front. An occlusion occurs when an atmospheric disturbance along a slow-moving cold front (or stationary front) causes a slight bend, or frontal wave, to occur. This wave strengthens and causes one section to move as a warm front and another section to move as a cold front. The peak of the wave develops into a low pressure system. The counterclockwise circulation around the low forces the two sections to move. An occlusion forms when the cold front overtakes the warm front.

## Occlusions

There are two types of occlusions: warm and cold. The warm occlusion occurs when the air ahead of the warm front is colder than the air advancing behind the cold front. When the fronts meet, the cool air rides up and over the colder air, forcing the warm air aloft.

The cold occlusion occurs when the air behind the cold front is colder than the air ahead of the warm front. When the fronts meet, the cold air replaces the cool air at the surface, again forcing the warm air aloft.

This powerful mixing of various temperature and moisture levels causes the occluded front to have the characteristics of both warm and cold fronts. In this situation, you have the opportunity to encounter a variety of clouds, from cumulus to stratus, embedded thunderstorms, precipitation from light to heavy rain, and hail and ice of all types. Much of the hazardous weather usually lies directly to the east of the occluded portion of the front. This band of poor weather can extend 30 to 100 miles ahead of the surface position of the occluded portion of the front.

As the occlusion matures and lengthens, it weakens to the point of becoming stationary and/or dissipating completely. Once stationary, it can remain in one area for several days. Occluded fronts are most common in the eastern U.S., again the result of moisture from the Gulf of Mexico.

## Dry lines

Dew point fronts (also called dry lines) occur when dry, dense air, such as that found over the Plain states southward into western Texas and New Mexico, meets moist air moving northward from the Gulf. There is little difference, aside from moisture content, between the two air masses.

Early morning and evening fog and low-level clouds mark the moist side of the front, while the dry side produces clear skies. Squall lines and tornadoes can form along this front in the spring and summer.

Sooner or later, an IFR flight will take you through a front. In addition to the cloud and precipitation already mentioned, you should be alert for several other changes which occur as you cross the front. These include changes in temperature, pressure, wind and dew point.

## Changes across a front

Temperature is the most noticeable change across a front, particularly if it is a strong cold front. The temperature change across this type of front is much more pronounced, so it's important to check the altimeter setting after crossing the front. Cold air causes the altimeter to read higher than your actual altitude. (Warm air causes the opposite effect.)

Pressure changes also occur, although not as noticeable as temperature changes. If you approach a front toward warm air, the pressure falls until frontal crossing is complete. It then remains steady or falls slightly the further you move into the warm air. When crossing a front into cold air, the pressure will rise, sometimes abruptly. Again, it's important to obtain a new altimeter setting after crossing the front. (Remember, high to low, look out below.)

Wind can always be expected to shift across a front. Passage of a front with no weather can be noted by a shift in wind flow and strength, and possible wind shear.

Finally, dew point differences can be noted across a front. These can help identify the front and can alert you to the location of fog and cloudiness.

During preflight planning, you can easily locate fronts by reviewing surface weather charts. Trends in the movement of fronts can be determined by requesting the charts from previous observation periods.

## Upper wind data

Don't ignore the upper wind information. The key to understanding fronts is in the upper regions of the atmosphere, since upper winds are the mechanism which form and move fronts. Carefully review the upper wind charts. Pay close attention to the movement and strength of upper winds, as these dictate the direction and speed of the fronts. When the upper winds parallel a front, the front has little movement. Wind blowing across a front causes the front to move with the wind.

Upper air troughs also play an important role in weather near the surface. Troughs, particularly when deep and coupled with surface fronts, can produce extensive cloudiness and widespread precipitation. Weaker troughs produce a narrower band of weather.

Anyway you look at it, crossing a front is not an enjoyable experience. It takes good planning to make it a survivable one.

# Year-Round Hazards

W hile many of the specific phenomena pilots encounter are strongly associated with either summer or winter weather (such as thunderstorms in the summer and ice in the winter), there's a lot you can run into at any time during the year (like turbulence or precipitation).

Before we go into detail on seasonal weather, let's take a look at these year-round phenomena.

## Precipitation

It was a typical July afternoon in New Orleans. ATIS Information Foxtrot was current: "...weather, two thousand five hundred scattered, two five thousand thin broken, visibility six miles in haze, temperature niner zero, wind two four zero at two, winds are calm, altimeter three zero zero one ...."

The first officer asked for a wind check as the crew of the B-727 taxied to the active runway. "Zero four zero degrees at eight knots," replied ground control. The controller advised another aircraft of low-level wind shear alerts in the northeast quadrants of the airport and provided relevant wind directions and speeds.

Another wind check was requested, to which the controller replied, "Wind now zero seven zero degrees at one seven, peak gusts two three, and we have low level wind shear alerts all quadrants, appears to be a frontal (sic) passing overhead right now, we're right in the middle of everything." The captain then advised the first officer to "...let your airspeed build up on takeoff..."

After liftoff, the aircraft reached an altitude of 150 feet agl and started to descend. The B-727 crossed the east boundary of the airport and crashed into a residential area. It was destroyed by the impact, explosion and subsequent ground fire.

A typical July afternoon in New Orleans. There were no sigmets, convective sigmets, severe weather warnings, local aviation warnings or severe weather watches in effect for the time and area of the accident. There were, however, level 3 cells over the airport and off the departure end of the runway which the flight crew scanned with their weather radar. The wind shear and heavy rain produced by these cells was strong enough to bring down a B-727 at takeoff power.

Even though no special weather advisories were issued, an understanding of the moisture content and stability of the air mass would have indicated what to expect from any weather encountered late that afternoon.

Water is constantly evaporating, condensing, sublimating, freezing and melting. The energy released at each transformation is significant and warms the air. The amount of heat generated by the release of one-half inch of rain over a square mile during a thunderstorm is 17 trillion calories, only 3 trillion short of the equivalent energy released by the atomic bomb dropped over Hiroshima.

Water becomes vapor through evaporation and sublimation. It is the constant fluctuation in the amount of vapor that concerns instrument pilots. This amount is measurable, so we can determine its effects. Two factors can be calculated by this measurement, relative humidity and dew point.

## Humidity and dew point

Relative humidity is expressed as a percentage and is calculated by comparing the actual water vapor content of air with the amount of vapor that could be present. Temperature is key to this calculation.

Warm air holds more water than cool air. The air becomes saturated when it cools and can't hold any more water. At this point, the relative humidity is 100%. (Any amount under 100% is considered unsaturated, but it doesn't feel that way on a humid summer day.) The air can cool to saturation when it moves over a colder surface; when stagnant air overlies a surface that is cooling down; and when the air expands as it moves upward.

The temperature at which the air becomes saturated is the dew point. When dew point temperature is compared to air temperature, you can determine how close the air is to saturation. The difference between the dew point temperature and the air temperature is called the dew point spread. The closer these two numbers are (the narrower the spread), the closer the air is to saturation.

When air temperature and dew point temperature are the same, the air is saturated and humidity is 100%. At this point, water vapor condenses or sublimates, using dust, salt or combustion by-products in the air for nuclei. These tiny droplets become fog (at the surface) or clouds (aloft). This can occur when the spread is five degrees F or less.

Predicting precipitation using the dew point spread is more difficult. For large droplets to form, the air must be saturated in several thick layers aloft. Once this occurs, precipitation is likely.

There are two ways precipitation can develop. In the first, water droplets grow by continued condensation or sublimation until they are too heavy for the atmosphere to hold. Then they fall as light drizzle, rain or snow.

The second method is more violent as the droplets collide and merge into larger droplets. Updrafts and downdrafts within the cloud keep the larger droplets suspended longer, so they continue to grow. Droplets that complete this process in mild air currents are likely to fall as light to moderate rain or snow. Droplets in strong up and down drafts have the most time to grow and fall as heavy rain, snow or hail.

Occasionally, the droplets remain suspended in clouds and retain their liquid state well below the temperature necessary for ice to form. This supercooled water is the cause of many an icing horror story. It is usually found in clouds between 0 and -15 C, where it freezes on contact. When it's colder than -15 C, sublimation usually occurs and ice crystals form.

## Precip changes

Condensation usually forms as rain or drizzle, while sublimation forms snow and ice crystals. Precipitation can change several times as it falls. Rain can fall through a cold layer, which produces supercooled water in the clouds and freezing rain below. It can freeze altogether and drop as ice pellets. Snow can melt while falling through a warm layer and turn into rain or freezing rain.

Hail is produced by frozen droplets that are suspended for long periods until growing to enormous size (golf ball to baseball size). When precipitation evaporates before reaching the ground, it is called virga.

For significant precipitation to form, the clouds must be at least 4000 feet thick, which gives water droplets room and time to grow. The heaviest precipitation usually comes from very thick clouds. Precipitation intensity can be an indication of cloud thickness along your route, but this is by no means an absolute indication.

Surface features influence the amount and type of water in the air.

Oceans and large lakes fill the atmosphere with water vapor, whereas mountain ranges trap the vapor, turning it into clouds as it is forced aloft. Be alert to the possibility of fog, precipitation and low ceilings any time the wind blows from water to land, and when the wind moves moist air upward.

The leeward areas of lakes are prone to fog, particularly when warm saturated air contacts a cooler water surface. In the winter, this is reversed when cold air moves over warm lakes. The Great Lakes are known for lake effect precipitation, especially during winter when snow can extend to the Appalachian mountains. Convective clouds also form on or off shore of coastal areas as a result of this process.

## Stability

It should be no surprise that the amount of saturation in the atmosphere affects air stability. As it moves, unsaturated air cools and warms at a fixed rate of 3 C (5.5 F) per 1000 feet. This rate is not affected by the temperature of the air mass through which it moves nor by heat released due to condensation. This process is called expansional cooling as the air moves upward and compressional heating as the air moves downward.

On the other hand, saturated air is affected by the temperature of the air mass, making the lapse rate more complex. As saturated air moves upward, it condenses and heat is released. This energy release partially offsets the expansional cooling, making the rate of cooling slower than in unsaturated air. Further, this rate is dependent on the dew point temperature and cooling is slower in warm, saturated air.

You may be wondering how this affects stability. When lifted upward, a parcel of surface air (unsaturated or saturated) can become colder or warmer than the surrounding air. If the air within the parcel becomes colder than the surrounding air, the air sinks (an indication of stability). If the air within the parcel remains warmer than the surrounding air as it rises, it continues to move upward as a convective current (an indication of instability).

The air inside the parcel cools at the fixed rate (3 C) as it rises, while the surrounding air cools at the ambient (actual) temperature lapse rate, which is 2 degrees C per 1000 feet. The difference between these two lapse rates determines whether the air is stable or unstable. (An inversion occurs when the lapse rates are reversed, so that the temperature increases instead of decreases with altitude.)

Any change in the ambient temperature lapse rate can change the stability. Cooling aloft or surface heating can cause instability (that's how air mass thunderstorms form on hot summer afternoons). Conversely, warming aloft and surface cooling causes stability.

Clouds are indicators of stable and unstable air. Convection is resisted in stable air, so clouds form into layers or strata. Aloft, these clouds become stratiform; on the ground they become fog. These clouds remain in layers as long as the air continues to be stable after condensation occurs.

## Estimating bases

The bases of cumuloform clouds can be estimated using the dew point spread. In a convective current, the rate of cooling of unsaturated air is approximately 5.5 F per 1000 feet and the dew point decreases at 1 F; therefore, the temperature and dew point converge at 4.5 F per 1000 feet.

To estimate the bases of convective clouds, in thousands of feet, divide the temperature/dew point spread by 4.5. For example, if the surface temperature is 88 F and the dew point is 70 F, the spread is 18 degrees. Divide 18 by 4.5, which means that the cloud bases will be 4000 feet. Use this formula only with clouds in unstable air.

Going hand in hand with the types of clouds is the ride you receive; smooth air (little atmospheric mixing) generally means stability, rough air (a great deal of mixing) means instability. Low ceilings and visibility are clues to stable air, as are widespread restrictions to visibility, such as fog, smog, haze and smoke.

Another clue of stability is temperature change. For example, if the temperature decreases rapidly as you climb, the air is unstable. If the temperature stays constant or decreases slightly with altitude, you're in stable air. If the temperature increases with altitude through a layer (inversion), that layer is stable, but the air may be unstable above and below it. Lastly, when air at the surface is warm and moist, you can bet the air is unstable. Any atmospheric change, such as surface heating, colder air moving in, or cooling aloft can lead to an outbreak of convective activity, and cumulus clouds.

Without moisture, there wouldn't be clouds or precipitation, and no need for instrument ratings. Flying in clear blue skies all the time would be easier, but boring. Fortunately, we don't need to worry about losing instrument proficiency.

*We'll talk more about various kinds of precipitation in later chapters.*

*Another major set of hazards that are not necessarily associated with a particular season concern turbulence of various kinds. While certain kinds of turbulent phenomena are strongly associated with thunderstorms (such as microbursts), turbulence is not necessarily a summertime-only problem.*

## Turbulence

It's annoying and dangerous. As with ice, it can catch you off-guard, with banged heads and knees the result of an encounter. In its fiercest form, it can destroy an airplane. It is difficult to forecast and occurs year-round. We could, of course, only be referring to turbulence.

Knowing the conditions which produce turbulence and what to do once you've flown into it increases your chances of escaping with only a story to tell.

Think back to your primary training days. It wasn't long before you learned that those bright mornings after frontal passage didn't always have smooth air for your lesson. The flight was plagued with bumps and jolts, which increased in intensity as the day progressed.

## Convective turbulence

Convective turbulence results from the sun heating the surface at uneven rates, due to variations in the surface. The air over barren areas such as parking lots, streets and plowed fields heats at a faster rate than the air over forests and lakes. The air eventually cools and descends at a slower rate. These ascending and descending currents—thermals—increase as the day progresses, causing glider pilots to rejoice.

Sunny summer afternoons, when accompanied by a calm or light wind, are prime time for convective turbulence (strong winds break up the currents). Turbulence strength is highly localized and its intensity varies with terrain. The layer of turbulent activity usually remains close to the surface.

With the passage of a cold front, on the other hand, the cold air moving over a warm surface also causes this type of turbulence, but the turbulent layer can extend several thousand feet upward.

If the heated air rises and cools to saturation, puffy fair weather cumulus form. The tops of the clouds indicate the top of the convective layer. Stay above the tops if you want a smooth ride. If the cumulus continue to build, they can develop into air mass thunderstorms. Air over deserts may be too dry for cumulus formation, but you can always expect plenty of unseen convective activity.

## Mechanical turbulence

Another type of turbulence is caused by air moving over and around man-made structures (hangars and other buildings on the airport) or natural terrain (single mountain peaks, ridges, hills and mountain ranges). This is called mechanical turbulence, because it results in a mechanical (brought about by friction) disruption of the wind flow.

The strength of mechanical turbulence is a function of wind velocity, building size and/or terrain roughness. High winds and rough surfaces combine to make for some really rough going. The wind also carries the eddies downstream and can produce the one gust that makes you lose control during takeoff or landing. Unstable air allows large eddies to form, but it can also break them up more quickly than stable air (where they dissipate at a leisurely pace).

Over mountains, stratocumulus are an indication of mechanical mixing. Found at the top of the turbulent layer, they usually line up in rows or bands, either perpendicular or parallel to the wind flow.

When wind velocity exceeds 40 knots, the turbulence can extend much higher than the tops of the mountains. Climb to an altitude at least 50 percent higher than the highest obstruction before reaching the mountains. Cross ridges at a 45 degree angle to cope with excessive updrafts and downdrafts. Wind speeds in the drafts can exceed the performance capabilities of your aircraft.

In a low valley, turbulence can be found near the leeward side of the mountain. In a narrow canyon or gorge, turbulence can be expected in the middle to downwind side. Stay near the side with the upslope wind, where you'll find additional lift. Avoid flight through high mountain passes and valleys during high winds due to funneling effects. Again, fly higher than or around these areas.

## CAT

Clear air turbulence (CAT) differs from convective and mechanical turbulence in that it produces a rhythmic pattern to the bumps and jolts, creating a washboard effect. It is usually encountered above 15,000 feet. This is the region of the tropopause, which separates the lowest level of the atmosphere (the troposphere) from the next highest level (the stratosphere). Jet streams are produced in breaks in the tropopause and are often the source of severe CAT.

CAT can also be encountered any time the upper air patterns produce wind shear. Some 75 percent of CAT encounters occur in clear air. High level cirrus clouds and haze layers often contain CAT.

High jet stream wind isn't always necessary for CAT. Sharp troughs aloft with speeds of only 20 knots can have CAT in or near the trough (typically in the straight areas of the U shaped trough) with the winds to either side of the trough varying as much as 90 degrees or more in direction. Also, wind circulation around a closed low can contain clear air turbulence (usually to the north of the low), particularly if the wind flow is merging together or splitting apart or is to the northeast of a cutoff low aloft.

## Vortex wake

No discussion of turbulence would be complete without mentioning of vortex wake turbulence. Wake turbulence is generated by the movement of an aircraft's wings through the air, which leaves a pair of counter-rotating vortices trailing behind. The strength of the vortices is determined by aircraft speed, weight and wing shape. It should be regarded as equally dangerous as the naturally occurring varieties, since vortex velocities can reach 130 knots.

The heavier, slower and cleaner an aircraft is, the greater the strength of the vortex. A hovering helicopter generates a prop blast similar to a fixed- wing aircraft. When moving forward, this prop wash becomes a pair of trailing vortices.

Vortices begin when an aircraft rotates during takeoff and continue until the nosewheel touches down during landing. Their circulation is outward, upward and around the wing tip, with the cores ranging in size from 25 to 50 feet across. They stay close together until dissipating. They tend to sink at 400 to 500 feet per minute, leveling off 800 to 900 feet below the glidepath.

During takeoff and landing, vortices sink into ground effect and move laterally across the surface at five knots. Crosswinds affect the direction of movement. They are slow to dissipate during low-level inversions.

If you aren't careful, significant structural damage can occur in wake turbulence. Recovery from a vortex-induced roll is determined by your aircraft's wing span and how control-responsive it is. If the wing span and ailerons of the larger, vortex-generating aircraft extend outward beyond the vortex, you can usually make an effective recovery.

To avoid wake turbulence en route, fly at or above a larger aircraft's flight path. When landing, land beyond a larger aircraft's touchdown point. When landing or departing behind a departing heavy aircraft, land or rotate the nosewheel before the larger aircraft's rotation point. A controller may alert you to the possibility of wake turbulence, but it's your responsibility to stay clear of it.

Turbulence occasionally bends an airplane. In many cases, structural damage to an aircraft is not directly the result of the turbulence itself, but occurs because the pilot loses control of the aircraft and, in attempting to recover, stresses the aircraft beyond structural limits.

Why do pilots lose control? Medical studies have shown that turbulence has a disturbing effect on the human body. It causes a pilot to react in a startled manner, delays decision time and produces involuntary control movements of which the pilot is unaware. It can also fool the senses, especially vision. Research indicates that when turbulence occurs at the rate of four cycles per second (which is extreme turbulence) visual acuity deteriorates. Instruments that may be indicating correctly cannot be read clearly and the pilot loses control.

## You can avoid encounters

You can prevent airframe damage by following a few guidelines. First, study the winds aloft reports. Wind speed variations of six or more knots every 1000 feet indicate possible moderate turbulence and 10 or more knots means it could be severe. Also study trends over your route; horizontal differences in wind speeds are another clue to possible turbulence, especially if the wind speed varies 40 knots or more at altitude over a distance of 150 to 200 miles.

An aircraft will react to turbulence according to its airspeed, weight, wing loading and pilot technique. (Aircraft with high wing loading usually tolerate turbulence better. The higher the aircraft speed, the more severe the turbulence will feel. Therefore, reduce to maneuvering speed (Va), or the speed recommended in the pilot's operating handbook for turbulence penetration.

Fly a level attitude. Do not attempt to maintain a particular airspeed or altitude. Call ATC and request a change in altitude and/or direction in order to leave the turbulent area as quickly as possible. Avoid abrupt control movements and make gradual climbs, descents and turns so as not to overstress the aircraft.

During takeoff and landing, you might carry more airspeed than normal in order to prevent a stall in a gust close to the ground.

Reporting turbulence is just as subjective as reporting ice. Severe turbulence to a Cessna 172 is light turbulence to a Boeing 737. But it is still important to report what you experience. Forecasters cannot measure turbulence, since it's often localized and rarely remains in one place very long. Forecasts for turbulence are based on factors such as wind velocity and terrain, but pilot reports are the best way of knowing where the turbulence is located.

Aircraft manufacturers build a great deal of strength into their products and it takes extraordinary circumstances to break them. Not losing control is the key to dealing with turbulence.

*This discussion touched briefly on a special kind of turbulence, the mountain wave. Though widely regarded as a Western phenomenon, mountain waves can also be found in the Eastern U.S.*

*The bad news about mountain waves is that they're powerful and violent, and can kill you easily. The good news is that they're predictable.*

## Mountain Waves

Mention mountain waves to any glider pilot and he'll tell you that they are a fantastic source of lift. To the powered aircraft pilot, mountain waves can be an unwelcome source of turbulence and hazardous flying conditions.

High season for mountain waves is October through April, when the general wind flow patterns of the colder months favor development.

Mountain waves, sometimes called lee waves because they form along the leeward (downwind) side of mountain ridges, develop when several factors are present in the atmosphere. These factors are a stable air mass above the mountain peak and a strong air current, at least 25 knots or more, blowing within 30 degrees of perpendicular (at or near right angles) to a mountain ridge.

The air mass above the mountains must be statically stable or an inversion must be present. Any sign of convective activity indicates unstable air, making wave formation less likely to occur.

Within the stable air mass, air flow remains in the same general direction with altitude and the wind velocity increases with altitude (a vertical wind shear). These phenomena usually characterize a front. While conditions favoring wave development often accompany frontal activity, the proximity of a front is not necessary for a wave to form.

Imagine a swift flowing stream of water as it tumbles over a bed of rocks and you have an idea of how mountain waves are formed.

## Wave characteristics

As a strong air current crosses the mountain peak, it descends sharply, as much as 5000 feet per minute, down the leeward slope. The air current then rises back up the crest several miles downwind, anywhere from eight to ten miles away. The wave crest, reaching twice as high as the mountain peak itself (perhaps into the lower stratosphere), then levels out and begins to sink again.

This wave motion can continue for as many as 10 or more times, losing strength and intensity as the distance from the ridge increases. Waves can extend downwind from a ridge by as much as 300 miles.

The wave's maximum amplitude (by definition, half the altitude difference between the wave trough and the crest) can be found at the maximum level of temperature inversion or atmospheric stability. This level can be anywhere from mountain peak height to the tropopause.

Amplitude varies with height above the ground, with maximum amplitude occuring at altitudes most frequented by jets; that is, in the upper troposphere (around 30,000 feet). Amplitude has a direct bearing on wave length; the greater the amplitude, the shorter the wave length.

Wave length, the horizontal distance between crests, usually ranges between two and twenty-five miles. Length of the wave is determined by the wind speed, being directly proportional to it, while also being inversely proportional to air mass stability.

The wave positions themselves remain stationary with respect to the ground, hence the term, "standing wave," provided the air current flowing through the wave continues to blow. Waves can remain in this state for hours, even days, before dissipating.

The intensity of mountain waves is generally much less over isolated mountain peaks than over long ridges, but a wave over a ridge can amplify and phase in with a wave formed over an isolated peak downwind, thus making the total wave motion much stronger, perhaps reaching into the tropopause or stratosphere.

## Cloud formations

Mountain waves can be detected by the distinctive cloud formations that often accompany them (Figure 2). A cap cloud often forms, looking much like a cloud waterfall flowing up over the mountain peak and down the leeward slope.

The sky is usually clear between the mountain peak and the roll or rotor cloud. The location of the first wave and each successive wave is marked by this turbulent cloud, which forms directly under the wave crest.

Its outward appearance is that of a "fair weather" cumulus or stratocumulus, with a base lower than the mountain peak and a top twice as high. However, looks can be deceiving. A roll cloud can contain dangerous turbulence and violent updrafts and downdrafts, with velocities of 70 to 100 feet per second!

The cloud will appear to remain in a stationary position over the ground as it constantly forms in the updraft and dissipates in the downdraft of the wave. Roll clouds can stretch in a continuous and stationary line downwind of the parallel to the ridge line.

## Lenticular clouds

Lenticular (lens or saucer-shaped) clouds often form above the wave crest. These smooth altocumulus clouds form in layers above the roll cloud, with the layers occasionally stacking up as high as 40,000 feet to the tropopause.

Updrafts and downdrafts exist on both sides of lenticular clouds, while turbulence can be encountered above and below them. However, the updrafts and downdrafts are not usually as violent as those found within a roll cloud.

Air moves smoothly in a laminar (non-turbulent) fashion in parallel streams within the lenticular clouds. Lenticulars also maintain a stationary appearance as they form in the updraft and dissipate in the downdraft of the wave.

Lenticulars will form within milder waves than that needed to form roll clouds and they are the best indicators of a wave condition. It is possible to see the wave length by noting the spacing of the lenticulars.

Lenticular clouds present in the middle and upper troposphere can be indentified from above even when an overcast hides lower level formations such as roll clouds. A very strong wave can be detected by looking for lenticular clouds arranged in successive rows downwind and stacked to higher altitudes.

An interesting characteristic of mountain wave lenticular clouds is that they often change shape and location in a matter of seconds, a characteristic that has led many ground observers to report them as UFOs.

Beware of using the clouds alone as indicators of wave conditions. Both roll and lenticular clouds may not always be present if the moisture content of the air is low.

## Turbulence varies

Not only can a wide range of turbulence be expected in these clouds, but also in and near a wave. The old rule of thumb that says you should fly at least 50 percent higher than the highest peak will usually keep you out of roll cloud turbulence, but you will still encounter turbulence created by the wave itself. A mountain wave can extend several hundred miles along a mountain ridge, so caution should always be used when approaching mountainous areas in wave conditions.

You can expect moderate turbulence from the surface to at least 10,000 feet which extends as far as 300 miles downwind. As the wave continues to build and strengthen, the smooth wave motion may break down and severe turbulence can result. High lenticulars with ragged and irregular edges are an indication that this breakdown has occurred. Severe turbulence can extend as far as 150 miles downwind of the ridge.

Surprisingly, flight in mountain waves that have long wave lengths can sometimes be relatively smooth. The only indication that you are in a wave may be slight fluctuations in altitude and airspeed. In addition, you will find the flight even smoother if you are flying upwind, as a result of encountering each wave at a slower groundspeed than if you were traveling downwind.

Mountain waves can pose a special problem for jet aircraft, that of an overspeed condition. When flying through a wave, a jet aircraft can exceed its maximum speed in knots/maximum speed in mach if updrafts of at least 3000 feet per minute are encountered when the aircraft is operating at its maximum aerodynamic ceiling.

## Wave locations

Obviously, somes areas of the United States have wave conditions more frequently than others. One such area is the Sierra Nevadas near Bishop, California, where the Bishop wave is located. This particular wave is well known for its high intensity. It is believed that the turbulence found within the roll cloud of the Bishop wave is the same as that found in most thunderstorms.

Other areas in the western U.S. where some of the strongest wave conditions are found include the northern and central Rockies and the Cascade mountains.

The coastal mountain ranges of northern California, Oregon and Washington also have their share of wave conditions. In these areas, cloudiness tends to obscure the wave formations, making them almost impossible to spot. The wind blowing from the sea over these mountains often produces waves of considerable strength.

In the eastern U.S., wave conditions can be found along the Allegheny, Catskill, Adirondack and White mountains. The southern Appalachians and the Ozarks also produce wave conditions, although these waves tend not to be as severe as those found in the western part of the country.

Predicting the location of mountain waves is not always possible, despite modern technology. Mountain ranges are complex in composition and the air flow over them reflects the terrain below.

## Precautions

Be alert for possible wave conditions when flying over mountainous terrain. A wave can occur without warning.

When crossing mountain ridges at lower altitudes, begin your climb at least 100 miles away. Give yourself plenty of altitude, at least 3000 to 5000 feet over the highest terrain. Approach the ridge at a 45 degree angle so you can make a rapid retreat if your aircraft is encounters a strong downdraft.

Depending on your type of aircraft and the altitude at which you fly, the ride will be smooth, to bumpy, to jolting. Common sense dictates that mountain wave activity should be avoided if at all possible. This can be as easy as a slight change in your flight plan, but remember to keep in mind the type of terrain that might underlie your new flight path.

*Another extremely dangerous hazard is wind shear. While most closely associated with thunderstorms, it can also occur as the result of other kinds of turbulent activity.*

*We'll discuss wind shear in detail here, and revisit the subject in the chapter on summertime hazards.*

## Non-Convective Wind Shear

Wind shear associated with convective weather may get all the bad press, but it's not the only kind there is. And it's not restricted to summer squall lines, either.

There are other conditions a pilot must evaluate for the presence of wind shear, e.g., low-level temperature inversions, frontal zones, mountain waves, etc. Although some conditions, such as mechanical turbulence, might not fit the strict definition of wind shear, the effect on performance is the same. Let's take a closer look at why these conditions produce wind shear, how to recognize these conditions before and during flight, and the adverse effects on aircraft performance.

### Temperature inversions

A low-level temperature inversion can form as the ground cools on a clear night with calm surface winds. At 800-1500 feet, the winds are 25 knots or more. Although invisible, eddy currents form in the shear zone between the two layers of air, creating turbulence.

With calm surface winds at night, you expect a smooth ride during the climb to altitude. Flying through an inversion layer surprises pilots who have not been attentive to wind and temperature variations on the surface and aloft. An encounter with turbulence at 600-800 feet indicates the presence of wind shear.

When the surface winds are light, takeoff can be in any direction, so the aircraft will climb through turbulent conditions and encounter either a sudden headwind or tailwind. The tailwind condition is less desirable since it will cause dramatic decreases in both airspeed and rate of climb.

You can prepare for a possible shear encounter by reviewing the winds aloft before flight. Look for the winds at 3000 feet to be at least 25 knots and then decrease in velocity at higher altitudes. When this occurs, and the temperatures aloft are warmer than the surface, wind shear should be anticipated shortly after takeoff.

Also make note of the winds aloft direction during the preflight briefing. Then plan your takeoff on a runway that will result in the maximum headwind component possible during climb-out, thereby avoiding the dangerous tailwind situation described earlier.

When descending through the shear zone, you could experience a sudden headwind increase while transitioning during a segment of a nonprecision approach or capturing the glideslope during an ILS approach. This is the classic wind shear encounter found in thunderstorm microbursts; the aircraft rises above the glideslope and the airspeed increases 10 knots or more. Your first instinct might be to reduce power and pitch the nose down. If you do, the aircraft will develop a tremendous sink rate as the wind diminishes.

## Frontal shear

Most pilots are familiar with the wind shear associated with cold fronts, but warm fronts also produce shear and are not as benign as once believed.

The shear hazards of cold fronts are present after the surface position of the front passes the airport. Some clues to its presence are a temperature change of 10 F or more across the front within 50 nautical miles and winds of 40 knots or more at 2000 feet above the surface. Shears of 40 knots in 200 feet are common in fast-moving cold fronts. When the front is slow moving, look for a large temperature difference across the front as an indicator of shear.

On the other hand, shear hazards with a warm front occur before the frontal surface passes the airport. The shear activity usually remains longer with a warm front due to its gradual slope.

## Methods of detection

Although wind shear is often difficult to detect until you're actually in it, there are several methods which can alert you to its presence.

If you fly the airplane by the numbers and consistently use a predetermined power setting and pitch attitude for airspeed and vertical speed while climbing or descending, you will immediately recognize a wind shear situation.

For example, you know that the airplane descends at 80 knots and 500 feet per minute with the pitch one dot below the horizon on the attitude indicator, and the power at 2000 rpm (assume a fixed-pitch propeller). When wind shear is first encountered in this configuration, the airspeed increases suddenly and the airplane stops descending.

Your first reaction may be to lower the pitch and reduce power, when instead, you should maintain the previous settings for the next minute or so. When passing through the shear, the aircraft may develop a high sink rate. Apply full power, if necessary, to arrest any excessive sink rate. Otherwise, adjust pitch and power as necessary to resume a safe descent to the runway.

A groundspeed indicator, such as DME or Loran, can also alert you when flying through a shear. When entering the shear, you will notice a groundspeed change of 10 knots or greater. This assumes that you were maintaining a constant airspeed before the shear encounter and the groundspeed indication is reliable.

If the groundspeed decreases, you are entering the classic headwind encounter and should respond accordingly. A tailwind encounter will result in a groundspeed increase and the rate of descent will also increase. In this case, you should increase power and adjust pitch as necessary to avoid getting dangerously low.

## Mechanical turbulence

Sooner or later, every pilot experiences the thrill of takeoffs and landings when the wind is blowing around buildings and other obstacles or across uneven terrain. The flare and touchdown in this situation demands good flying technique to avoid a bent airplane. This form of turbulence is known as mechanical since the disruption of the wind flow is the result of objects on the ground, or the ground itself. It also produces shear which can affect aircraft performance.

A strong wind blowing across uneven terrain around an airport creates shear conditions which should be anticipated during takeoff and landing.

For example, if the wind is blowing over terrain which slopes down to the runway, the result is a downdraft that degrades climb performance during takeoff. This is not a good situation in which to depart a short runway with the aircraft fully loaded. The airplane will probably require a longer ground run and the rate of climb will be less than indicated by the performance charts in the pilot's operating handbook. It's a good idea to have excess power available in case climb performance deteriorates.

Landings can also be challenging in this situation. If the wind is blowing up a hill from the runway, an aircraft descending on final encounters an updraft. This results in a delayed flare and overshoot if there isn't enough runway available.

If the wind is blowing down a hill from the end of the runway, you can anticipate a downdraft on final, which could result in an undershoot if you do not react quickly. Be prepared to go around when this condition or the one in the previous example exists.

A good mountain flying course will improve your flying skills and understanding of the effects of wind shear on aircraft performance when dealing with mechanical turbulence and mountain waves. Flight through wind shear can also be practiced in a simulator, should you have access to one which can duplicate this meteorological phenomenon.

*The last of our general weather phenomena is one that may surprise you: lightning. Like wind shear, it's commonly associated with thunderstorms.*

*However, lightning can occur at other times and in other places. It may be a rare hazard, but it's one to watch out for nonetheless.*

## Lightning

When you think of lightning, what image comes to mind? Besides the bright flash, you might envision dark, boiling clouds, gusty winds and deafening thunder. All are ingredients of nature's most dangerous creation, a thunderstorm.

Would it surprise you to learn that lightning frequently occurs in nimbostratus and other stratoform clouds, as well as in mixed precip?

Many surprising discoveries resulted from the National Aeronautics and Space Administration (NASA) Storm Hazards Program, which is based at the Langley Research Center in Hampton, Virginia. The program started in 1977, the result of a recommendation from the National Transportation Safety Board to investigate thunderstorm-related phenomena. NASA gathered lightning data between 1980 and 1986 in a modified two-seat F106B Delta Dart. Bristling with special instrumentation and one-of-a-kind photographic equipment, the F106 was hit 714 times during its mission lifetime.

## Classic lightning

Charged ice crystals and water droplets collide within a cumulonimbus cloud. Just as your body builds up a charge as you rub your feet against a carpet, the cloud becomes charged by a separation of electrical charges. Positive charges are carried into the top of the cloud and the negative charges collect at the bottom. These charges are released in an electrical discharge—lightning.

Lightning can occur within the cloud (intracloud), cloud-to-ground, or between clouds. Over the life of a storm, approximately 70 percent of the lightning generated is intracloud.

It was common belief that the freezing level, within plus or minus eight degrees, was the altitude at which an aircraft had the greatest chance of being struck by lightning in a thunderstorm. In reality, the higher you go above the freezing level, the more likely it is that the aircraft will be struck. The aircraft's intrusion into the highly charged regions of the cumulonimbus clouds will actually trigger a strike.

According to Bruce Fisher, project engineer for the Storm Hazards Program, "Triggering predominates at the higher altitudes in over 90 percent of the strikes we encountered. Down around the freezing level, the strike rates are much lower." The greatest number of strikes occurred at altitudes where the temperature was -40 C.

## Aircraft induced

An aircraft can trigger a strike by flying into an electrical field. (All clouds carry a weak electrical field, but thunderstorms more so).

The many sharp points on an aircraft, e.g., antenna, wingtips, propeller tips, etc., increase the local electric field that surrounds the aircraft as it enters a cloud. The field is stressed at these points, causing a localized breakdown, and an electrified streamer is generated which attaches itself to the aircraft at one or more of the points. The streamer (or streamers) propagates away from the aircraft and generates a discharge—a lightning strike—triggered by the aircraft itself.

The lightning channel is stationary. The aircraft continues forward, but is still attached to the channel at the points. As the aircraft travels forward, any attached streamers at the front of the aircraft "walk" or sweep backward toward the rear of the aircraft. It, and any other streamer, are strung out behind the aircraft for several hundred feet, leaving long luminous trails, until the ends of the streamers connect with pockets of charge and the channel dies out. The entire process takes about one second.

Inside the aircraft, you might not be aware of the strike. In large aircraft, such as commercial or military jets, "the effects are so benign, you may not know it, unless it strikes in the field of view of the crew," said Fisher, "or if you hear a loud bang." Another tell-tale sign may be burn marks on the airframe.

In general aviation aircraft, however, it could be a different story. "In most cases, again, nothing will happen, except, maybe, a bright flash or loud report, enough to startle you," stated Fisher. "There are usually no critical electric systems to worry about on board most smaller general aviation aircraft, but keep in mind that avgas is very volatile. If you get a spark, you can get an ignition leading to fire or explosion. It's also possible to receive an uncomfortable shock, especially whoever is holding the controls. At night, you could suffer momentary flash blindness, which may result in temporary loss of control of the aircraft."

## Precipitation and turbulence

Another shattered belief is that lightning only occurs in areas of heavy precipitation and turbulence.

"We found," Fisher said, "that at both high and low altitudes (above and below a mean of 20,000 feet) that 80 to 85 percent of the lightning strikes were associated with negligible to light turbulence and precipitation. That was another big surprise." The team also found that precipitation and turbulence in a thunderstorm don't necessarily go hand in hand. "But," Fisher warns, "understand that the test pilots still experienced high levels of both precipitation and turbulence while in the clouds, but when the strike occurred, either triggered or natural, the aircraft was in a lull. We still don't fully understand the interrelationship between these three hazards."

You might be thinking at this point that lightning strikes can be avoided by flying around ominous looking cumulonimbus clouds. According to Fisher, who has participated in a number of lightning-induced accident inquiry boards, it can snake out of a thunderhead and take a bite out of your aircraft from 20 to 50 nm away while in visual conditions.

In February 1987, a NASA T-38 was struck "several miles" away from a thunderstorm. The crew stayed out of the clouds to avoid icing, and the aircraft was hit while in the clear. A fuel tank ignited, creating a fire, but the pilot landed successfully.

"This is why you'll see Federal Aviation Administration (FAA) advisory circulars suggesting you stay at least 20 nm away from the visible cloud boundary. This doesn't mean the contour on radar, but the visible cloud itself," says Fisher.

## Other occurrences

Lightning strikes occur in other conditions besides thunderstorms. The Storm Hazards team, using data from ongoing thunderstorm research and operational data from commercial airlines and the military, found most aircraft strikes occur in nimbostratus and other stratoform clouds, in mixed precipitation (rain, sleet, and snow) and while flying at or around the freezing level in these conditions.

Although more research is needed in this area, non-thunderstorm lightning is known to occur in cold weather—early spring, late fall and winter. "Pilots will not see any other lightning, and the ride will be smooth. Then they may see a light flash or hear a loud report. That's it. They got into a weak ambient field in the cloud and triggered a single discharge," says Fisher.

In these cases, no airborne instrument (weather and doppler radars, or lightning detectors) will warn you, since there is no natural lightning to look for, no turbulence and light precipitation. "Lots of people call this a static discharge," said Fisher, "but there's no such thing. A static discharge simply will not cause the kind of damage we've been talking about."

## St. Elmo's fire

The eerie glow that sometimes appears at night on the windscreen, wingtips or propeller, St. Elmo's fire is precipitation static, not lightning. Although St. Elmo's fire cannot build to cause a discharge, it occurs in the same environmental conditions as lightning. Says Fisher, "If you see St. Elmo's, or hear static on your radio, or your ADF goes crazy, consider it a warning that you're in an area where there's a chance you'll get a strike. Fifty percent of all strikes are associated with the presence of St. Elmo's fire."

## Composite structures

The increased use of composite material in aircraft and the new digital "fly-by-wire" control systems concerns many researchers.

Most of today's aircraft are aluminum, which is an excellent conductor of electric current. This allows current to slip along the outside skin and shields the inside from harm. Composite material, on the other hand, resists electric current, causing dangerous electromagnetic fields to build up inside the aircraft. Without proper shielding, considerable losses in equipment and possibly lives can occur, particularly where the digital control systems are concerned.

"That illustrates one of the reasons we got into the lightning business," recalls Norman Crabill, former manager of the Storm Hazards Program and now an independent consultant. "Fly-by-wire systems can be vulnerable to erroneous commands generated by lightning pulses." What worries Crabill and other lightning researchers is the use of the digital systems in composite aircraft, particularly fiberglass homebuilts, that are not designed to handle a lightning strike.

"A composite airplane, with a digital system, while it may be efficient and economical, if it gets struck, may be uncontrollable," Crabill warns.

Composite aircraft with digital controls have been certificated by FAA, for example the Beech Starship. The FAA requires all aircraft undergoing certification to withstand peak current charges of 200,000 amperes (which is what a "superbolt," a powerful cloud-to-ground strike might generate). The strongest recorded hit taken by the F106B was 54,000 amperes; however, Fisher believes the aircraft received hits of at least 100,000 amperes. Cautions Fisher, "It's easier to design in the shielding from the start than to add it later. This remains as area of real concern to us."

## Vertical Lightning

Although lightning research at Langley has ended, it continues with experiments conducted by the U.S. Air Force, the National Severe Storms Laboratory in Norman, Oklahoma, the FAA Technical Center in Atlantic City, New Jersey, and others. At NASA's Marshall Space Flight Center in Huntsville, Alabama, researchers are hunting for lightning on a global scale using satellites. Among other things, they're looking for an elusive phenomenon called vertical lightning.

According to Otha Vaughn, one of the Marshall researchers, "It comes straight out of the top of the storm aimed at the ionosphere, up 2,000 to 4,000 feet, with tops of the clouds anywhere from 15,000 to 50,000 feet. It seems to occur in very strong storms, the kind you see in the midwest or northwest areas of the U.S."

Vertical lightning is rarely observed because it is impossible to see it from the ground. Reports about it actually go back about 30 years, mostly from airline pilots who have seen it once or twice. It is of particular interest to NASA because of the vulnerability of the Space Shuttle to lightning strikes. Marshall researchers are also working on a lightning mapping/detection system using satellites. The system will track storm paths and shed some light on the global patterns of lightning.

Some big questions about lightning still remain to puzzle researchers. For the sake of those of us flying near the stuff, let's hope these questions get answered soon.

# Summertime Hazards

While most of the winter hazards we'll be covering in the next chapter are strictly cold-weather problems, many of the phenomena associated with summer can occur during cooler months, as well.

Still, you're far more likely to encounter events like thunderstorms and microbursts when the air is warm, moist and unstable...those conditions that summer is made of.

In the last section we looked at some strategies to avoid severe summer weather, and some ways to survive an encounter if one does happen. Now, we'll examine in detail the weather itself, beginning with the number one threat: thunderstorms.

## Thunderstorms

Cells. Cbs. Cumulonimbus. Convective activity. Any way you describe them, thunderstorms spell trouble for the pilot any time of year, but especially during the spring and summer.

Under the right conditions, thunderstorms can occur just about anywhere on the planet, even in the cool arctic regions. In the continental U.S., however, they are most common during the spring and summer, when there's plenty of atmospheric lifting action and lots of moisture, the two main ingredients needed to cook up a thunderstorm.

Yet even though most thunderstorms form under similar conditions, not all cells are created equal. When and where a thunderstorm occurs has a lot to do with how intense it will become and how long it will last. And if you're not radar-equipped, visually avoiding some thunderstorms is out of the question.

Compared to forecasting ice and turbulence, the state of thunderstorm forecasting is really quite good and getting better. The NEXRAD doppler radar is capable of pinpointing cell development about an hour before it actually happens and within a few miles of the actual location.

Good as they are, though, thunderstorm forecasts don't give the pilot the big picture. For that, it's helpful to have some background knowledge of the geographical nature of thunderstorms, a kind of thunderstorm atlas.

## Recipe for trouble

Regardless of where they form, the recipe for all thunderstorms is the same: moist air, lifting action and an unstable atmosphere to keep the air rising once it has started upward. Just how that lifting occurs— whether by convection, orographic lifting or by frontal activity—is a geographic variable in thunderstorm development. That, in a nutshell, is why summer thunderstorms in the dry desert southwest aren't like those in the southeast during the springtime.

When the lifting process is vigorous enough, a would-be thunderstorm enters the first stage of its development, the cumulus stage. During the cumulus stage, as the air rises and cools, latent heat from water vapor condensing into droplets (and eventually ice crystals) is released. The released heat further accelerates the upward motion of the air, with updrafts reaching velocities as high as 3,000 feet per minute.

As the rising air reaches the tropopause (from 12,000 feet to 60,000 feet MSL) it has cooled off so much that it becomes dense and heavy enough to begin descending. This creates the second stage, the mature stage. At this point, rain (and sometimes hail) falls from the base of the cell. The second stage is when the most intense storm activity—rain, turbulence, lightning, hail—takes place. Downdrafts of up to 6,000 feet per minute are possible.

During the final or dissipating stage, the updrafts have ceased so there is no longer enough latent energy to sustain the storm. Downdrafts continue to develop while the updrafts weaken. If there is no strong wind shear in the upper atmosphere, before the cell dissipates, there will be a period when most of the motion is downward.

Any remaining updrafts tend to be suppressed by the intense downdrafts. If there is a strong wind-shear with increasing velocities as altitude increases, the storm cloud "tilts." Under these conditions, up- and downdrafts aren't aligned and don't collide so there's no self-canceling effect. In this case, the mature stage is longer and may continue as long as the cell is fed by updrafts ascending outside the cloud boundary.

## Four flavors

Most pilots are familiar with the six-level method used by the FAA and NWS to classify precipitation intensity from radar echoes. Quite apart from that, meteorologists break thunderstorms into four very general classifications, which are only points in a continuous spectrum of sizes and shapes. The list includes single-cells, multi-cell events, supercells, and squall line events. All but the supercell have severe and non-severe varieties, depending on intensity. A supercell is always classified as severe. To qualify as severe, a storm must have at least one of these phenomenon: wind gusts greater than or equal to 50 knots; hail 3/4 inch or larger, or tornadoes.

The single-cell is actually fairly rare in the U.S. These storms usually develop through all three stages within 20 to 40 minutes. But just because they are short-lived, doesn't mean they are benign. A single-cell can have a short period of severe weather including microbursts at the surface. It was a severe single-cell that brought down a Delta L-1011 at Dallas-Fort Worth in 1985.

A recent safety report given to U.S. Air Force aircrews listed these visual clues to understanding the single-cell thunderstorm. A "tilted" storm shows a strong wind shear of at least 50 to 60 knots at altitude. If there is vertical development after an initial tilt in the thunderstorm, the storm is intensifying and more likely to produce severe weather. How would you tell if shear is present? A long anvil cloud is a good clue. It suggests that the storm is being tilted by strong shear and being fed by strong updrafts.

The multi-cell storm is actually the most common variety of thunderstorm. These storms have from two to four separate cells in different stages of development. Because they are competing for moisture and energy, multi-cells tend to negate one another and prevent the storm from reaching severe intensity.

The whole multi-celled complex will be steered by the upper atmospheric winds in which it is embedded. As viewed with your back to the wind, the individual cells will propagate on the right flank of the complex while older cells to the left are dissipating. This process has been described as a pulsing motion. Under the right conditions, multi-celled events become part of a much larger phenomenon called Mesoscale Convective Complexes (MCC). These monsters can grow to more than 1,000 miles in length.

Many of the same visual cues that apply to single-cells apply to multi-celled storms. A weak storm will have a shorter updraft which tilts downwind. A severe storm will rise more vertically and develop an overhanging cloud at about the 20,000 to 30,000 foot level. Downbursts tend to start on the leading edge but shift to the trailing flank.

While the multi-celled storm has individual cells that pulse to life and then decay, the supercell is a single-cell in the mature stage whose updrafts and downdrafts support each other in an equilibrium state rather than clashing and dissipating. These storms are always severe. They usually form when there are strong upper atmospheric winds and a turning low-level wind that creates an updraft rotation. The updrafts become so strong that they actually "punch through" the tropopause to become an "overshooting top" in the stratosphere.

The up- and downdrafts are so strong in this type of storm that the whole cell acts like a mountain to obstruct mid-level winds flowing around it. These winds form eddy currents downwind and a strong secondary downdraft behind the cell. This downdraft, which may be in the clear, can produce severe turbulence.

Usually, the supercell will have an almost vertical updraft turret. A wall cloud can develop at the rear edge of the storm. Finally, the heaviest rain and hail will fall near the trailing edge of the storm, that is, on the upwind side.

The final storm type is the squall line. This is simply a solid or a broken line of cells in a thin band. The line can be made up of single-cell, multi-celled or supercell storms or combinations of all three. Even though a supercell is usually an isolated or small clustered event, when it does appear in a squall line, it's usually the southernmost cell or a cell at an eastward bend in the squall line.

The structure of the squall line puts the severest updraft on the downwind side rather than the upwind. Because of the outflow that moves ahead of the squall line, there's very severe turbulence ahead of this type of storm system. However, it's a common misperception that the severest weather occurs in a squall line. Actually, the supercell can claim that dubious distinction.

## Brewing up a storm

So where are the thunderstorms? It depends on the time of year, moisture available, the local atmospheric stability and what kind of lift is available. Obviously, moisture comes from humid regions so it's no surprise that thunderstorms are most prevalent there. The general prevailing winds are important at the 700 millibar level (roughly 10,000 feet) in the west and the 850 millibar level of the atmosphere in the east during the summer months, the prime thunderstorm season in the U.S.

Examining the atmosphere at these relatively low levels is important because this water-bearing air is carried aloft to begin and sustain the creation of a thunderstorm. Much of the moisture that kicks off thunderstorms in the midwest and even the east comes from the Gulf of Mexico. This moisture-rich air is carried in ("advected" is the buzzword) from the subtropical gulf as far northward as the Great Lakes. Pacific Ocean air is not very important to thunderstorm development because the coastal mountain ranges block its flow inland. The Pacific is also cold off the west coast so that the air flowing inland is not really very humid.

A second source of moisture comes from the surges of maritime tropical air that enter southern Arizona and California from the Gulf of California and the tropical Pacific during the summer, especially when dying tropical storms find their way to the northwest coast of Mexico.

Now for the lifting mechanisms. There are many ways for a parcel of air to rise. Convection—heated air rising—is one. Orographic lifting—a moving air mass encountering rising terrain—is another. Frontal, squall line and air mass are three others.

Any type of front (cold, warm, stationary, or occluded) can produce lifting and a thunderstorm. Since a cold front tends to have a steeper gradient of cold air wedging under a warmer air mass, it has very active lines of storms, usually during the afternoon. Stationary front thunderstorms tend to be widely scattered while a warm front tends to produce the weakest thunderstorms (usually isolated) because of the gentle slope of warm air riding up over a cooler air mass.

Squall-line storms develop 50 to 300 miles ahead of the advancing cold front in moist, unstable air. Here again, a severe clash of cold and warm air force moisture upward.

Probably the most dangerous thunderstorms are those associated with the occluded front. In this scenario, a significant clash of different air masses encourages lift, creating well-established thunderstorms. Unlike the cold-front thunderstorms, which sometimes stand alone in relatively clear air, occluded front storms are frequently embedded in stratiform clouds and are usually difficult to see. This makes them difficult to avoid without radar or Stormscope.

Air-mass thunderstorms form in a warm, moist air mass but are not frontal. Three primary methods produce these storms: convective heating from the land below, converging airflows forced upward and orographic lifting.

## A Cb atlas

It's possible to generalize about how different lifting forces and moisture work together to create thunderstorms across the continental U.S. Along the west coast there are very few thunderstorms because of the cold California Current flowing along the coast. True, air forced up the

Sierra Nevada range does occasionally give birth to a storm but whether these are thunderstorms is open to debate.

In California's central valley, conditions are often right for a weather observer to see lightning but never hear the thunder. Technically, a storm is not officially a thunderstorm unless thunder is heard. What's probably happening is that the thunder is reflecting off a temperature inversion above the valley. I've seen several California weather observations that had in the remarks section, "Cb overhead, lightning observed."

During spring, the continental landmass is still generally cool and the sun is moving higher in the sky. Thunderstorms are common only in the southeastern U.S. where the warm, moist gulf air moves north to clash repeatedly with the colder continental air in wave after wave of frontal activity. As the season progresses, this clash tends to take place further and further north. Land-sea breezes also blow along the coastal areas. This provides lifting action along the shore and it's why thunderstorms are very common in the spring and early summer off the Atlantic coast, particularly around Cape Hatteras. These are almost always air mass thunderstorms.

During the summer months, the continental U.S. experiences its primary thunderstorm season. Frontal activity moves to the northern portion of the country. In addition, monsoonal moisture now flows in from the Gulf, through the southwest, and is forced aloft by the Rocky Mountains.

This produces a thunderstorm maxima in the United States along the lee side of the Rocky Mountain Ranges. In Denver, the period of peak activity occurs between 2 p.m. and 4 p.m. These are orographic storms. As they move eastward, they may kick off air mass thunderstorms which develop into multi-cell and supercell storms as the day progresses. These also occur in New Mexico, caused by the intense orographic influence of the San Juan Mountains.

As the orographic cells born in the Rockies move east, they often intensify, producing an evening or night time storm maxima in the lower great plains. By the time the storms cross Kansas, they've been fed by convective currents and Gulf moisture to reach a peak in Kansas by about 8 p.m. Squall lines and supercells form and become self-sustaining. They continue to grow as they move east. These large storms last for another six to 12 hours, often developing into the massive Meso-Scale Convective Complexes we described earlier.

In the southeastern U.S., there's also an afternoon convective maxima. The Florida landmass shows the extreme case where by day the land heats up to create a large-scale sea breeze that brings in moist air from over the Gulf. Convection driven air-mass thunderstorms are the general rule in the southeast and in the upper Great Plains.

## Forewarned and forearmed

So how can you as a pilot know when the next thunderstorm will strike? The answer to that comes with knowing where to look. Obviously, the area forecast along with local terminal forecasts will tell if thunderstorms are expected. But this is as common a feature of summer forecasts as ice is in winter so it isn't all that helpful.

The radar summary chart is probably the primary tool and certainly the most specific for thunderstorm information. It gives actual location, size and shape of cells. By looking at the directions of movement and the velocities of individual cells and clusters, and by corroborating this with the wind at the 500 mb level which steer the storms, you'll have some idea of what to expect from the larger storm systems.

Although we said earlier that the thunderstorms are not difficult to forecast, Dr. Wayne Sand, a National Center for Atmospheric Research scientist, explains that thunderstorm forecast confidence is not high. The best a professional forecaster can manage is something like "a 40 percent chance of thunderstorms in Eastern Colorado."

Sand's advice to pilots is to talk to the locals. Find out where and when storms predictably form, and where they move. Cells often follow surprisingly predictable patterns. In addition, look at the temperature and dew point. Anytime the dewpoint is high (above 55 degrees) or if temperatures are high with a small dewpoint spread, storms are likely.

You can quantify the forecast by calculating K-factor, the relationship of temperature to dewpoint. You'll need from FSS (or DUAT) the temperatures and dewpoints at 500, 700 and 850 millibars. The formula is simple: add the temperature and dewpoint at 850 millibars to the dewpoint at 700 millibars. From that sum, subtract the temperatures at 700 mb and then add the 500 mb temperature.

A K-factor of less than 15 indicates very low likelihood of storms. At 25, the chance is 40% or less; at 26 to 30, expect a 60% probability; 36 to 39 means a 90% likelihood of storms. The K-factor is a useful guide to severity too. If a storm should happen to occur in an area of low K-factor, the chances of it being severe are quite high. This is because the cells will build to very high altitudes where the rising air will be chilled, creating intense downdrafts and microbursts.

*In the last chapter we talked about wind shear caused by forces other than convective activity. Now let's take a closer look at wind shear caused by thunderstorms.*

## Convective Wind Shear

Heavy weather was in the area as the flight crew of the Lockheed L-1011 was being vectored for an approach to the Dallas/Ft. Worth Airport. Visual approaches were in use until an arrival controller announced, "...there's a little rainshower just north of the airport and they're starting to make ILS approaches...tune up 109.1 for one seven left."

"We're gonna get our airplane washed," remarked the first officer. After issuing a final vector to join the localizer, the controller cleared the flight for the ILS to Runway 17L. One minute later, the controller broadcast, "And we're getting some variable winds out there due to a shower...out there north end of DFW."

Moments later, "Lightning coming out of that one," said the first officer. "What?" asked the captain. The first officer repeated "Lightning coming out of that one...Right ahead of us." As the approach continued, the captain cautioned the first officer to watch his airspeed when rain started pelting the windscreen.

"You're gonna lose it all of a sudden, there it is," warned the captain. Seconds later, the captain exclaimed, "Push it up, push it way up. Way up! Way up! Way up!" The sound of engines at high rpm were heard as the captain said, "That's it."

Despite the admonitions of an experienced captain, the first officer failed to add sufficient power in time to arrest the increasing sink rate, and the airplane crashed 30 seconds later.

This accident, and others related to thunderstorms, usually come to mind when pilots discuss wind shear. The fact is, wind shear plagues more pilots than those flying "heavy iron," and in many conditions other than thunderstorms. It can also be encountered after a cold front passes, before a warm front passes, and in conjunction with sea breeze fronts, mountain waves and strong surface winds.

Some pilots believe that wind cannot affect their airplane in flight except for drift, groundspeed, etc. Obviously, this cannot hold true if the wind changes faster than the aircraft can accelerate or decelerate. Wind shear is a sudden change in wind direction and/or velocity over a very short distance. Let's begin reviewing this phenomenon in nature's scariest wind shear producer, a thunderstorm.

## Terminology

Downdrafts, downbursts, microbursts and gust fronts are associated with thunderstorms. These terms are often misused and are important to understanding how wind shear is created.

A downdraft is a strong flow of cold air that moves rapidly downward in a mature thunderstorm and is caused by falling precipitation.

A downdraft is what you typically associate with a thunderstorm; that is, a column of cold air which spreads out beneath the thunderstorm when it reaches the mature stage. A downdraft descends through the storm, then spreads out along the surface, sometimes as far as 15 miles. A large dome of rain-chilled air results, and the surface pressure inside the dome of cold air is higher than the air surrounding it. This is the reason for rising barometric pressure as the thunderstorm passes by.

This cold-air dome moves out ahead of the storm. On the ground, you feel a strong gust of wind which shifts direction and an accompanying drop in temperature, both of which signify a gust front—another form of wind shear.

A localized, intense downdraft with vertical currents exceeding a downward speed of 720 fpm is considered a downburst. This velocity approximates the climb rates of many aircraft, making an encounter extremely critical during takeoff or landing. The downburst diameter is usually three to four miles aloft and can affect an area 15 miles in diameter after striking the ground.

A microburst is a downburst less than three miles in diameter and does not spread far upon surface contact. Within the microburst are extremely tight wind shear gradients. The changes in wind speed and direction are so rapid and closely spaced that an airplane penetrating a microburst might not be able to recover.

Microbursts are smaller versions of downbursts, but can be just as powerful. A microburst is short-lived, from two to 20 minutes, while it affects an area on the ground of less than two-and-a-half miles. In a large thunderstorm, it can be the start of a gust front. The strongest microburst recorded in the United States occurred at Andrews Air Force Base, on the heels of a landing by Air Force One. The surface winds were clocked at 130 knots, followed by a shift and a measured velocity of 84 knots, a range of over 200 knots!

Microbursts can occur any time a thunderstorm is present. The frequency of microbursts increases in two atmospheric environments. One is an extremely dry environment in which moist convection is barely possible. The second is an extremely wet environment that produces microbursts embedded in heavy rain.

## Dry air

In the west and southwest U.S., extremely dry air causes cumulus clouds to build from high bases, 2.5 miles above the surface. Below this high cloud base lies a dry layer, with surface temperature/dew point spreads greater than 30 degrees F.

In these dry conditions, any precipitation that falls evaporates before reaching the ground (known as virga). The clouds may appear fibrous and often have developed anvils. Lightning is not always present.

You can encounter a microburst in this seemingly benign setting, but there are some visual clues. Consider any virga falling from the cloud bases as a sign of a potential microburst.

If the virga is accompanied by a swirling ring of dust at the surface, don't fly through this area: the invisible dry microburst is in the middle. The dust ring is created by the vortex circulation of the air surrounding the base of the microburst. The dust ring won't be present if the ground is wet.

Large dry-line thunderstorms (not associated with frontal activity) can produce virga and dry microbursts very far from the main body of the storm and its corresponding radar echoes. This makes use of present-day radar unreliable in spotting microbursts.

High-based clouds can also produce heavy precipitation in a dry environment. High-based thunderstorms with heavy rain signal a deep, mixed stability layer, with a high lapse rate and enough falling precipitation to start a strong downdraft.

## Wet environment

In a wet, moist environment, the bases of cumulus clouds form at lower altitudes, bringing potential microbursts (embedded in rain showers) closer to the surface. The wet environment is marked by a saturated lower layer, topped by an elevated dry layer. A wet, or embedded, microburst is difficult to spot, but there are visual clues. Rain showers often create a shaft-like appearance when falling from cloud bases. Where a rain shaft nears the ground, an embedded microburst develops a foot-like protuberance that extends outward and to one side of the shaft, moving far forward under a rain-free portion of the cloud.

This is caused by strong winds at the base of the rain shaft that push the precipitation beyond the shaft's edge. This wind may even kick up a small cloud of dust or dirt as it moves forward. The tip of this foot, (made visible by dust or water droplets) curls up and back, lifted by the swirling vortices of the microburst.

Narrow rain shafts may not have the foot-like evidence, but instead may have wispy upward curls at the shaft's edge at the surface. The curls are sprays of raindrops caught in the vortex of the microburst.

Another indication of a strong downburst that could develop into a microburst is a rain shower with an opaque-looking base. A downburst conveys rain toward the surface much faster than in still air. As the downburst nears the surface, it decelerates and allows a heavy accumulation of water just above the ground, causing the opaque appearance at the bottom.

A descending wet microburst can appear as a darkened globular mass of heavy rain moving through an area of light rain. The rain is carried downward much faster than possible in still air. The microburst collects the water droplets as it descends, becoming visible by the developing mass of water.

## Intermediate environment

Microbursts can also form between the two extremes of wet and dry. In this intermediate environment, characteristic around the Gulf of Mexico, microburst potential increases when the following atmospheric conditions exist: high convective activity; little or no capping inversion; a dry adiabatic lapse rate layer, at least 5,000 feet deep, below the cloud condensation level; a moist layer between 5,000 and 15,000 feet; and an elevated dry layer above 15,000 feet.

The visual clues used to spot a microburst in the extreme environments also work well in the intermediate environment.

## Preflight briefing

Between March and October, terminal forecasts often contain the phrase "chance of thunderstorms," even though there may not be a cloud in the sky. Knowing that wind shear occurs in and around convective activity, what questions should you ask during a weather briefing to determine if it will be a factor during your flight?

Although the radar summary chart may be uppermost in your mind, there are two forecast products you can discuss with the FSS specialist or weather briefer that will be especially helpful, the stability chart and the convective outlook.

## Stability chart

The stability chart helps predict possible thunderstorm activity by outlining areas of stable and unstable air, plus the moisture profile of that air, across the country. This is accomplished by calculating two numbers, the lifted index and the K index, which appear as a fraction on the chart.

Stability is indicated by the upper portion of the fraction, known as the lifted index. This is calculated by "lifting" a parcel of air to 18,000 feet. A positive lifted index means that this parcel of air if lifted would be colder than the surrounding air at 18,000 feet; therefore, the air is stable. High positive values indicate very stable air.

A zero index means that this parcel of lifted air would be the same temperature as the air at 18,000 feet. The air is neutrally stable (neither stable or unstable).

Be careful when you see negative indexes on the chart. This means that the lifted air is warmer than the surrounding air at 18,000 feet and unstable, ripe for convective activity. Large negative values indicate very unstable air.

The lower portion of the fraction on the chart is the K index, which reflects the temperature and moisture profile of the atmosphere. These two elements allow the meteorologist to judge the stability of the air. Although computation of the K index is rather involved, it can best be summarized by saying that a large K index indicates conditions favorable for air mass thunderstorms, as a result of an unstable lapse rate and moisture-laden air.

For easy reference, the contour lines on the stability chart connect lifted index values of +4, 0 and -4. Meteorologists also highlight unstable areas with a U and stable areas with an S.

A high probability of severe thunderstorms exists with a lifted index of -6 and a K index of 35 or greater. The National Weather Service classifies a thunderstorm as severe when it has 50-knot or greater surface gusts, three-quarter inch or larger hail and/or tornadoes.

## Convective outlook

If you aren't crazy about discussing lifted and K indexes over the telephone, the convective outlook can help determine the risk of severe weather along your route.

The convective outlook (AC) is issued daily at 0800Z and 1500Z, and an additional outlook is prepared at 1930Z from February 1 to August 31. These forecasts are valid until 1200Z the next day, and highlight areas of the country where there is a high, moderate or slight risk of severe thunderstorms.

A typical AC could read as follows:

**THERE IS A MDT RISK OF SVR TSTMS THIS AFTN AND EVE PTNS ERN AL..ERN TN..ERN KY..WV..PA..NY...**
**GEN TSTM ACTVY TO RT OF LN FM MLU MEM TOL...**

When deciphered, these paragraphs mean:

"There is a moderate risk of severe thunderstorms this afternoon and evening in portions of eastern Alabama, eastern Tennessee, eastern Kentucky..."

"General thunderstorm activity to the right of a line from Monroe, Louisiana, Memphis, Tennessee..."

This example indicates a moderate risk of severe thunderstorms, meaning that these thunderstorms could cover 6-10 percent of the affected areas. A high risk would cover more than 10 percent of the indicated areas, and a slight risk would cover 2-5 percent.

After reviewing the stability chart and the convective outlook, you will have a better understanding of the conditions which could create convective weather as well as an indication of the severity of that weather.

## Inflight updating

Keeping abreast of thunderstorm activity once airborne can be difficult if you do not have storm detection equipment on board. Contacting Flight Watch on 122.0 MHz can be helpful. The briefer often has access to "real-time" weather radar and/or current satellite imagery, both of which indicate how rapidly the convective activity is developing and the intensity.

Do not rely on air traffic control radar to help pick your way through lines of thunderstorms. Remember, this radar filters out all but the most severe weather in order to display aircraft returns in spite of weather. Even though a controller may be able to keep you out of the most severe activity, there could be other weather hazardous to your aircraft which is not depicted on the controller's display.

Fly at an altitude where you can observe building cumulus and avoid these clouds when possible. When available information indicates that this activity has formed into lines, seriously consider landing and waiting awhile, or be prepared for a wild ride.

## Detection difficult

Like a stall at low altitude, wind shear must be recognized and responded to immediately for a safe recovery. However, it is not always easy to detect, and this is especially critical during takeoff and landing. Even the low-level wind shear alert systems installed at some airports cannot detect all of the wind shear associated with thunderstorms, due to the transient nature of microbursts.

Although wind shear reports from other pilots are desirable, do not rely on them as your sole source of information. A report from someone who took off or landed ahead of you may not be of help, even if that report is only one minute old. Also, the absence of wind shear reports does not indicate the absence of wind shear.

## Microburst indicators

The following indicators, when present with convective activity,

should alert you to the presence of microbursts and wind shear:
• Rapidly building or changing cumulonimbus activity
• Heavy precipitation
• Lightning
• Virga
• A temperature/dew-point spread greater than 30 F
• Blowing dust on the surface

## The encounter

When flying through a downburst during landing, the aircraft will first encounter a headwind, then downburst, and finally a tailwind.

For example, you have the power set and the elevators perfectly trimmed to maintain 90 knots and a 500 fpm descent with the needles centered on the ILS. Suddenly, without changing anything, the airspeed increases 10-15 knots, the aircraft stops descending and you are well above the glideslope; the first indication that something is amiss.

Your first instinct might be to reduce power and lower the nose to recapture the falling needle. Moments later, as you fly through the downburst and ensuing tailwind, the descent rate pegs out at 2000 fpm and the airspeed decreases dramatically. If full power is not applied immediately, you may find yourself out of altitude, airspeed and ideas all at the same time.

Most light aircraft can develop full power quickly to compensate for the loss of lift caused by the downburst, provided the power is applied as soon as you recognize the encounter. Larger aircraft, however, require longer engine spool-up time, which often makes recovery difficult. It is not unusual for microburst velocities to reach 1500-3000 fpm, a condition which makes recovery doubtful when flying below 1000 feet agl.

In the unfortunate event you encounter a downburst or microburst during takeoff, apply all available power. This is no time to worry about exceeding the maximum power limits. Maintain a climb attitude and continue straight ahead. Do not attempt a 180 degree turn back to the runway.

Wind shear is insidious, since no fool-proof method of detecting it exists. Know the indicators and be prepared, particularly when operating below 1000 feet agl. The best precaution is to delay the flight if on the ground, or, if airborne, to divert to a safer area. When wind shear conditions exist, never assume you can make the takeoff or landing safely, even though everyone else appears to be operating normally. This assumption has resulted in tragedy for a number of pilots.

## Recovering from an encounter

Microbursts should be avoided, regardless of the environment in which they form. Many air carriers thoroughly train their pilots in downburst/microburst recovery techniques.

However, many general aviation pilots aren't as fortunate when it comes to adequate training for a microburst encounter. Here's what you can expect if you're caught in one:

• Your airplane encounters a headwind as it penetrates the spreading outflow of air from the microburst. If you're landing, descent slows or stops and the airspeed suddenly increases as much as 15 knots.

• Next, the aircraft encounters the rapid downward force of the microburst and then almost immediately experiences a tailwind. The descent rate can be 2,000 fpm or more and the airspeed will rapidly decrease.

Resist the initial instinct to reduce power and lower the nose when you first encounter the downburst. Instead, apply full power as quickly as possible. Maintain a level climb.

If you encounter a microburst on takeoff, maintain a climb attitude and don't even consider returning to the runway. Your chances of success in this situation aren't great unless you have lots of excess power available. A microburst can out-gun a Boeing 747.

Delay your takeoff or arrival if factors indicate microbursts in the area. Remember, a microburst usually passes quickly, in 10 to 15 minutes. Don't rely solely on controllers to warn you and don't rely on other aircraft that have landed or departed safely.

The installation of Terminal Doppler Weather Radar (TDWR), which can accurately detect downbursts/microbursts, is currently underway at many airports, with more to come within the next few years; it will improve your chances of avoiding an encounter. Since every airport won't have this equipment, your best bet is to observe and use your knowledge of weather conditions.

*Thunderstorms aren't the only hazard associated with the summer environment. Another is high density altitude, which is bad enough in itself...coupled with convective activity it can be a killer.*

*Poor visibility, air mass thunderstorms and high density altitude are dominant features of summer weather. Since an encounter with at least one of these is likely, here's a review of the conditions and how to cope with them.*

## Summertime Blues

"No problem," said the pilot as he loaded his family into the airplane.

A quick check of the weather revealed no change; the haze and heat prevailed. The briefer kept repeating, "Chance of thunderstorms...."

"Not to worry," said the pilot to his kids. "We'll be at the beach long before they pop." Visibility was poor, but that's why he had an instrument rating.

"No time for a weight and balance. I know how much I can stuff in my airplane," said the pilot to himself. During run-up, the engine was running hot. Quick, firewall the throttle and away we go.

The airplane wasn't accelerating fast enough and the end of the runway was coming up. Beads of sweat stood on his forehead as he nursed the overloaded airplane over the trees. But that wasn't the end of it. Visibility was worse than expected and a few of the buildups dead ahead had lightning.

## Smog and haze

Smog and haze are the leading culprits of poor visibility, especially when a high pressure system stalls over an area, allowing the air to stagnate. Haze and smog are particles of salt, dust and combustion by-products suspended in an atmosphere that has little movement.

They form in layers and can extend from the surface to as high as 15,000 feet, but most layers have definite tops only a few thousand feet high, above which you can often climb and fly in the clear.

The major hazard with haze comes when flying or landing into the sun, since downward visibility is poor. To estimate slant visibility, look at the ground over the nose. The visibility is approximately one mile for each 1000 feet of altitude. Unless you arrive at your destination when the sun is higher in the sky, plan on flying an approach. Beware of others trying to sneak in VFR.

## Air mass thunderstorms

Air mass thunderstorms are particularly hazardous when embedded in a haze layer, making them difficult to spot. Once they mature, they may cluster or form into short squall lines. Check with flight watch for the latest information. If you don't have radar or Stormscope, ATC radar can be used as a last resort to determine the location and direction of movement of any severe weather.

Air mass thunderstorms are short-lived and often self-destruct within an hour. The falling precipitation and downdrafts cool the bottom of the clouds and the underlying surface, thereby cutting off their source of energy. Don't underestimate their punch, as they are just as vicious as the frontal variety of thunderstorm. It pays to give them wide berth.

## Density altitude

Pressure and humidity, as well as temperature, determine air density. Density altitude is pressure altitude corrected for nonstandard temperature. The standard temperature at sea level is 59F (15C) and the standard pressure is 29.92 inches of mercury. Any time the conditions differ from the standard, aircraft performance changes.

Pilots flying from sea level airports often fail to consider density altitude, which is an index of aircraft performance. High density altitude reduces the performance of your aircraft, sometimes to the point where it can't make it off the runway.

Expect reduced power as the engine takes in less air, reduced thrust as the propeller has less air to bite into, and reduced lift as the lighter air puts less force on the wings.

Density altitude doesn't show up on the airspeed indicator. Indicated airspeed remains the same. What does change is true airspeed and ground speed, which increase as density altitude increases.

High density altitude affects performance at cruise. If the air is warm, the service ceiling of your airplane is lower, a serious consideration, especially when flying in mountainous terrain.

## Operating guidelines

Because of the severe effects of density altitude, plan to make some changes in your normal operating procedures.

• You're asking for trouble if the aircraft is at gross weight. Reduce fuel, passengers or baggage when density altitude is high. Always check the performance charts to be sure you have enough runway to takeoff and clear obstacles.
• Consider changing the time you depart or land to the coolest periods of the day.
• Unpaved, short and/or sloped runways with obstacles make the density altitude situation much more complex. Most POH takeoff charts assume a paved, level and dry runway.

There are two rules of thumb for takeoff: For each 1000 feet above sea level, takeoff run increases by approximately 10 percent; and for each 1,000 feet above sea level, true airspeed on landing will increase by approximately two percent (indicated airspeed stays the same). Also, for normally aspirated engines, 30 percent of horsepower is lost at 10,000 feet and 40 percent is lost at 14,000 feet.
• Keep ground operations, such as taxiing and run-up, to a minimum. Avoid continuous start-ups and shut-downs. Point the nose into the wind as much as possible.

• For a normally aspirated engine, consider leaning the engine to maximize your performance. Follow the procedure in the pilots' operating handbook.

Summer brings special conditions. Due to increased traffic, hazy days around popular airports require extra vigilance. The possibility of air mass thunderstorms should be reviewed. And calculating density altitude, something many pilots continue to forget or ignore, should be a standard part of your flight planning.

# Wintertime Hazards

For most of us, winter is one great big pain in the neck. Short days, freezing temperatures, and sloppy weather conspire to cause us real problems. Not least among these are the hazards we face as instrument pilots. In their own way, winter hazards are more insidious than those found in hot weather. While thunderstorms are big, noisy, and obvious, the primary problem in winter—icing—can sneak up on a pilot without his realizing how bad the situation is...until it's too late.

We'll start this last chapter with a look at icing, and how it affects your airplane.

## Icing

The Cessna 182 bucked as he attempted to maintain control. The stall warning horn wailed and his wife grabbed his right arm. They were solid IFR for at least an hour and the ice (unforecast) that accumulated on the wings, struts and windscreen was causing the airplane to descend. He applied full power and was still descending! If only he could get to warmer air. He should have turned back at the first sign of ice, but it was Christmas, and they just had to get home. He picked up the mic and called ATC for assistance, but it was too late....

No one should have to tell you about the dangers of structural icing. Aviation publications are full of accounts of highly skilled pilots losing control of their aircraft due to ice. Flight instructors regularly drum into our heads to never, ever fly through clouds containing the substance.

So why do even experienced pilots get into trouble? It's usually inadvertent due to lack of proper planning. In many instances, it is a lack of understanding about what ice can do to an aircraft.

Contrary to popular belief, it is not the weight of ice that causes ice-related accidents. Weight is increased and must be considered a factor in the overall effects of ice, but a slight increase in weight pales in comparison to what happens to the aerodynamic qualities of the aircraft.

Once ice has developed on an airframe, even in amounts as little as one-half inch, lift can be decreased by 50 percent and drag increased by at least 15 percent. Stall speed can increase by as much as 30 percent or more as the angle of attack needed to produce the stall is reduced at the same time. Fuel consumption also increases as the airplane struggles to keep flying.

Sooner or later, if you fly IFR, you're going to encounter ice. Therefore, it is essential that you understand what ice is, how it forms, what it can do to aircraft and what you can do to cope with it.

## Three classifications

Icing can be classified into three groups, depending on where it is found and how it is formed: in-cloud, precipitation and other (frost, induction, etc.).For ice to form on your aircraft while in the clouds, several factors must be present: moisture (in the form of liquid water), freezing temperatures and an object large enough and fast enough to accumulate ice.

The amount of ice that accumulates is directly related to the amount of liquid water found in the cloud; the more liquid present, the larger the potential ice accumulation. Common sense tells you that anything already frozen, such as ice crystals or dry snow, is not as likely to stick to an aircraft while it moves through the clouds as something more fluid. In some instances, ice forms by sublimation; that is, it goes directly from vapor to ice.

## Droplet size

Liquid water in clouds forms into droplets, with the size of the droplets varying between 10 and 50 microns. (1000 microns equals one millimeter and 25.4 millimeters equals one inch.) For our purposes, let's say small and large droplets. Droplet size plays a key role on the shape and amount of ice accumulation.

As your aircraft enters a cloud, it sets up a disturbance in the cloud's pressure field, which causes a wave to form ahead of the aircraft. (In actuality, every component of the aircraft creates its own little pressure wave in front of it.) This wave parts the airflow, which then slips around the aircraft. The liquid water droplets that form the cloud are caught in this movement. The smaller droplets are carried away from the structure by the airflow, but the larger ones are not carried away and impact on the structure. Generally, the larger the droplets, the more ice accumulation.

The size and speed of the collecting object also affects the amount of ice that forms. You might believe that the larger the object, the more ice will accumulate. Actually, the opposite is true, due to the fact that a large jet aircraft will create a pressure wave much farther out in front of it then a single-engine aircraft. The extended pressure wave gives the water droplets, particularly the larger ones, traveling in the airflow more time to get out of the way. Larger droplets have difficulty avoiding smaller objects, so items such as pitot tubes and antennas accumulate ice very quickly.

On the other hand, the speed of the object changes accumulation rates in a slightly different manner. The faster the object, the less time the pressure wave has to push the droplets, large and small, out of the way; hence, more ice collects. (Keep in mind that slowing down is not the thing to do when ice accumulates on the airframe. The more time you spend in the cloud, the more ice will collect.)The air temperature is also an important ingredient for an icing encounter. Icing occurs when the outside air temperatures are between 0 and -10 C. Rarely will you accumulate ice at temperatures below -20 C. Of course, there are exceptions. Icing has been known to occur when temperatures are as high as 4 C and as low as -25 C.

It's interesting to note that jet aircraft can often escape or minimize ice accumulation in flight due to the process of aerodynamic heating (heat created by the friction of the air moving over the aircraft surface). The amount of heat required to prevent ice can only be generated at speeds of 400 knots, which is not practical for most aircraft. Don't assume that jet aircraft are immune to ice. We have seen accident reports indicating that even jets can be vulnerable.

## Ice shapes

The shape of ice on aircraft surfaces also contributes to decreased performance. These shapes vary from a smooth, clear glaze to a bumpy popcorn appearance. Two types of ice are responsible for this variety—clear and rime.

Clear ice forms when large, relatively warm (close to freezing) droplets hit a surface then run back to freeze behind the point of impact. This process can, over time, build up ridges of ice that form double-horn or butterfly shapes which play havoc with the aerodynamic qualities of your airplane. Clear ice is extremely heavy, is usually clear in appearance and is very difficult to dislodge in flight.

Rime ice forms when small, supercooled droplets (colder than the outside air but remain in a liquid state until striking an object) strike the surface and freeze on contact. The ice then builds on that spot into a cone or spearhead shape. The characteristic milky or opaque appearance is due to air bubbles trapped underneath the surface of the ice. Rime is much more brittle and a bit easier to remove in flight (with the proper equipment) than clear ice, but it should be considered equally dangerous.

In the real world of weather flying, it is probable that you will pick up a mixture of these two types of ice. In general, clear icing occurs between -1 and -5 C, mixed occurs between -8 and -10 C and rime between -11 and -15 C.

Regardless of the type that attaches itself to your airframe, remember that the more critical areas of concern are the amount of accumulated ice and its shape.

## Cloud types

Stratus and cumulus clouds can produce both types of ice; however, the formation of these clouds predisposes each for a particular type of ice.

The most severe icing is found in clouds with high liquid water content. It will come as no surprise that this factor is usually found in cumulus clouds. The same atmospheric lifting conditions that create cumulus also collect tons of water in the process.

If the temperature at the cumulus cloud bases during the developing stage is around -12 C, the clouds are wet and have the potential for heavy icing throughout. Cumulus cloud droplet size is much larger than stratus clouds, so you should expect large amounts of clear ice at and above the freezing level.

Horizontally, icing levels are not very extensive in cumulus, so the actual time in icing is relatively short. The worst icing in cumulus is found over mountains, in frontal systems, in thunderstorm formation and in cumulus formed over open water, wherever high convective activity occurs.

Over mountainous areas, the most severe icing can be found in cumulus above mountain crests and to the windward side of the ridges.

In frontal activity, freezing temperatures can be found at all levels in both cold and warm fronts. Cold fronts generally produce clear ice due to the predominance of cumulus clouds and due to freezing rain. Warm fronts, which usually generate stratus clouds, produce rime ice in the overrunning warm air segment. (Although cloud tops in winter warm fronts rarely extend above 20,000 feet, a climb can expose more aircraft surface to ice accumulation. Only climb if absolutely necessary.) If overrunning warm air is unstable, expect clear ice in the resulting cumulus.

## Icing in CBs

Icing in thunderstorm cumulus occurs at different levels as the cells develop, mature and dissipate. When developing, severe icing can be found above the freezing level. When the temperature in the cloud tops is -20 C, ice crystals appear as the supercooled liquid changes its state.

In the mature stage, droplets in updrafts are liquid above -10 C, are mixed with ice between -10 and -20 C and turn to ice crystals below -20 C. In downdrafts, droplets are mixed liquid and ice from 0 to -10 C, with mostly ice crystals.

As the storm enters the dissipating stage, most of the droplets turn into ice crystals, except for a shallow layer near the freezing level, where a mixture of liquid and ice frequently exist.

## Stratus clouds

Stratus clouds usually have less severe icing due to decreased vertical activity to distribute moisture. Cloud droplet size is small and you can expect rime ice.

Icing layers in stratus are often less than 3000 feet thick, with the largest drops and highest water content found near the cloud tops. The horizontal distribution of ice will extend for greater distances, but usually less than 30 miles. (This is not true in lake-effect formations in the Great Lakes. Icing in these clouds can be quite extensive as they are generally much wetter in content than typical stratus, due to their origin over water.) If the cloud base temperature is less than -3 C, rapid ice accumulation in stratus is less likely to occur.

Stratocumulus clouds should be treated slightly different than stratus. The slight convective nature of these clouds can create severe icing in the areas of highest convective lifting and near the cloud tops.

Precipitation icing, which includes freezing rain and drizzle, is quite different than cloud ice. The very mention of freezing rain and drizzle should send chills down your spine. An aircraft that can fly for an hour through normal cloud ice can be totally disabled in seconds by these two forms of ice.

Freezing rain and drizzle are caused by precipitation falling through air that is slightly above freezing into air slightly below freezing. The liquid droplets become supercooled and freeze instantly on contact with an object.

Water droplet size in freezing rain is much larger than most droplets found in clouds: 1000-5000 microns (3175 microns equals 1/8th of an inch). Freezing drizzle droplets average 100-300 microns. These are much larger than cloud droplets.

With drops this large, an airframe can be coated rapidly and completely. More often than not, it is the unprotected surfaces that accumulate the most ice, such as the undersides of the airfoils and fuselage.

Visibility in freezing rain can also deceive you into believing it is safe to fly. Three to four miles visibility is normal in freezing rain. Freezing drizzle, on the other hand, is often accompanied by fog. Be alert to below freezing temperatures when flying through fog.

Both warm and cold fronts produce freezing rain and drizzle, depending on the side of the front in which you are flying. It will most likely occur when flying in the colder air masses of both fronts.

## Snow

Snow is another form of precipitation icing which can create its own brand of mischief. You can generally assume that when the temperature is around -20 C and you are clear of clouds, snow will not stick to the airframe.

Snow can pass through areas of warmer air on the way down and melt. Occasionally, these half-melted flakes pick up a coating of ice and turn into snow pellets. These pellets love to stick to anything in their way, e.g., windscreen, airfoils and propellers.

In general, consider any snow cloud a potential ice generator, especially when the temperature is between -12 and -20 C (which is a prime condition for rime ice).

## Frost

Ground ice, or frost, and induction icing are forms of icing that do not receive as much attention as they should. Frost is definitely a concern before takeoff, but it can also occur in flight.

Frost is a thin layer of ice that forms on most exposed aircraft surfaces when (in a process similar to dew formation) radiational cooling occurs at night and the surface temperature is below freezing. During flight, frost can form on upper and lower surfaces when a descent is made from subfreezing air into a warmer, moist air mass. The moisture comes into contact with the supercooled aircraft skin and frost, or a thin clear glaze, coats the structure.

The effects of frost can be just as deadly as a solid, thick coating of ice. Frost on an airfoil can give the surface enough roughness to reduce lift and increase drag. A heavy coating of frost can increase stall speed five to ten percent. Performance can be drastically reduced to the point where the aircraft cannot become airborne during takeoff. Removal before flight is essential, as is the removal of any other coating of ice or snow that may be on the aircraft.

## Engine ice

Induction icing should also concern you since it can adversely affect engine performance to the point where the engine quits. It can occur anytime during the year, whenever moisture and freezing occur.

This type of ice forms in the air intakes of an engine. It occurs when the downward moving piston of a piston engine or the compressor of a turbine engine forms a partial vacuum at the air intake. The air expands adiabatically as the vacuum cools the air. When the temperature drops below freezing and sufficient moisture is present, sublimation causes ice to form on the intake. The ice starves the engine of oxygen. The fuel, as it evaporates, can produce additional cooling.

Methods of handling induction icing are dependent on the aircraft. Familiarize yourself with the proper technique prior to flight by consulting the engine operating guide for your aircraft.

## Root causes

Just as with thunderstorms, ice requires an understanding of weather formation to make an intelligent go/no-go decision. The object is, after all, to avoid the stuff in the first place, so knowing ahead of time what causes it can keep you from making a bad mistake. The four elements of weather that pilots should understand are:
• Moisture
• Temperature
• Stability
• Lift
Let's review each element and how it should be analyzed during the icing season.

## Moisture

The first item to check is moisture, since without it, you can cross ice off the worry list. Start by looking for weather systems that draw moisture from large bodies of water, such as the Pacific Northwest, Atlantic Coast, Great Lakes and Gulf of Mexico. Once you know where the moisture's coming from, find out where it's going. Weather systems create icing conditions hundreds of miles from the moisture source.

Next, check the temperature and dewpoint on the surface and aloft. The temperature/dewpoint is easily obtained from surface observations and winds aloft reports provide upper air temperature, but what about the dewpoint aloft? This can be obtained from a series of seldom-reviewed observations known as constant pressure analysis charts.

Constant pressure analysis provides observations at the following pressure levels (the altitudes are approximate):
- 850 mb - 5000 feet
- 700 mb - 10,000 feet
- 500 mb - 18,000 feet
- 300 mb - 30,000 feet

Temperature/dewpoint spread at these altitudes gives a hot clue to the air's moisture content. A spread of less than 5C indicates moisture-laden air and a spread of 2C or less indicates a high probability of ice at the right temperature.

The ideal temperature for ice formation is 0 to -10C and it will continue to form down to -20C. Find out if these moisture-laden and temperature sensitive areas are moving in pockets or in wide-spread areas. It may be possible to underfly or overfly ice-filled layers. Always know where there's a clear area, just in case.

Constant pressure charts are produced twice daily at 1200Z and 0000Z. They aren't normally requested, so be patient (but insistent) with the briefer when getting this information.

## Stability and lift

Air stability and lifting are as important to understanding icing conditions as they are to understanding thunderstorm severity. These two elements determine the type of clouds and ice you'll encounter.

The greater the lift, the wetter the clouds. Treat building cumulus at icing temperatures as you would severe thunderstorms. These clouds are highly liquid and temperature at the cloud bases is -12 degrees C or warmer.

On the other hand, stratus clouds usually have icing that is stratified in layers 3000 feet or less. The highest liquid water content and largest droplet size is in the top of a stratus deck. The exceptions are the northwesterlies over the Great Lakes, westerlies in the Pacific Northwest and northeasterlies off the Atlantic Coast. In these cases, ice can be encountered at all altitudes in stratus clouds.

The stability panel of the composite moisture stability chart is the best source of stability and lifting information. Like the constant pressure charts, it's available at 1200Z and 0000Z daily.

Don't overlook the lifting effects of terrain. Wind flowing over the mountains from a large body of water creates moisture-laden wave clouds filled with ice directly over and downwind of the ridges. A recent frontal passage and wind from a moisture source are often precursors of this condition.

Naturally, you should ask for pilot reports to confirm the presence of ice and cloud tops. Don't be lulled into a false sense of security due to a lack of reports. Many pilots don't report icing encounters to flight service because they're too busy dealing with it.

Once airborne, ask each controller if anyone has reported an encounter. You can also ask the controller to query other aircraft further down your route.

Most importantly, always have an alternate plan in the event things go sour when ice is even remotely possible.

## Ice advice

It usually is not any single factor, but several in combination, which produce structural icing. In general, if you want to avoid an encounter, stay out of it, on the ground. If you get into it anyway, get out as fast as possible. A small fast-moving object collects far more ice in a shorter time period than a large slow-moving object. The shape of the ice, once it builds, plays a large role in destroying the aerodynamic qualities of your aircraft.

*Let's take a close look at how to get a good briefing for ice. It's a bit tougher than when looking for convective activity, since icing conditions don't show up on radar like thunderstorms do.*

*We've included a practical example in this section to show just what to look for on the charts, should you have access to them.*

## Briefing for Ice

Winter flying carries its own set of challenges and risks, one of which is the ever-present possibility of an encounter with ice. Answer these five questions during your briefing and you'll know what to expect:
• Where's the moisture?
• What's the temperature?
• How stable is the air?
• Is there any lifting?
• What is the speed and movement of the air mass?

## Where to start

Along with current surface observations, closely review the adverse conditions in the area forecast. This covers significant clouds and weather, flight precautions, icing and freezing levels. Then look at the weather depiction and radar summary charts to get a big picture of the weather.

If you can't get these charts, have the briefer review them for you, watch A.M. Weather, or, as a last resort, look in the newspaper. Remember that data on these charts can be several hours old, so always refer back to current observations and forecasts.

Go beyond the bare minimum with your briefing—the standard read-out of synoptic weather, the current and forecast conditions, notams and ATC delays—offered by the briefer if you want to stay clear of ice. This information is useful and has a place in your planning, but, in icing weather, it pays to take the time to investigate conditions further. The final decision rests with you, not the briefer.

Thanks to modern technology, weather information regarding current conditions is reliable. It's more difficult to forecast where that weather will be in the future.

The standard briefing will no doubt include some mention of icing conditions, even if there is only a slight possibility of it developing. This is the FAA's way of telling you that there is known icing, and flying through known icing is a definite no-no, unless your aircraft is certificated to do so. If you fly the average-equipped airplane (which is not certificated for known icing), you risk a violation, provided you live to tell the tale. If you plan on remaining below the freezing level and/or clear of clouds, tell the briefer that this is your intention, so you're on record in the event something happens.

## Four items to check

You don't have to be a meteorologist to ascertain where the ice will be (remember, the briefer isn't a meteorologist either). There are four items you must check along your planned route: where the moisture is located, the temperature in these areas, the air-lifting agents present and the stability of the air. You should be looking for the conditions conducive to ice formation.

Begin by checking the freezing level chart, which indicates the altitudes above which you can expect icing. Then check the various constant pressure (millibar) charts. (If you can't review these in person, ask the briefer to cooperate and review them for you.) A review of these charts should include the 850 millibar chart, which lists the observations at approximately 5000 feet over the reporting stations, and the 700 millibar chart, with observations at approximately 10,000 feet msl. If you plan to fly higher, review the 500 and 300 millibar charts (approximately 18,000 and 30,000 feet msl respectively).

Reporting stations are indicated on the charts by small circles.

Weather data is listed next to each station. A shaded station circle represents an observation of a temperature/dewpoint spread of five degrees C or less, a sure indication of moisture-laden air. Check the temperature at that station. If it is between 0 C and -20 C, there's an excellent chance that ice is present in the clouds at that altitude.

## Look for indicators

Before you growl and trash your flight plan, check the observations at other altitudes. It is possible to avoid ice by flying at an altitude where temperature and moisture will not produce ice (though there are no guarantees).

You should also look for indicators of instability, such as an overrunning air mass, cold or warm. The composite moisture stability chart (known formerly as the stability chart), which shows the location of stable, unstable and neutrally stable air, and radar summary and surface analysis charts should be checked. High convective activity produces lots of moisture and sopping wet clouds.

In order to establish trends, ask to review the charts from the previous reporting period or periods, if available. Note the previous position of the area of moisture and determine if the size or moisture content of it has changed. Where is the area moving? Does your planned route take you near or through it?

Pay close attention to wind speed and direction, as this is the mechanism for the movement of moisture. Winds aloft observations are included on the millibar charts and appear as small barbs extending from the station circle.

Be alert for areas where the winds are moving over land from areas of open water. The largest ice-producing clouds can be found along the Pacific northwest coast, along the eastern edge of the Great Lakes and along the east coast when winds blow easterly off the Atlantic Ocean. Sources of moisture can also come from the south. East coast residents can thank moisture originating in the Gulf of Mexico for many snow and ice storms.

Finally, you should be aware of the lifting agents that will affect the moisture, sending it high into the atmosphere where it condenses into various forms. As you may have already guessed, frontal activity provides plenty of lifting. Be careful if your planned route crosses one.

Mountainous terrain also provides tremendous amounts of lift. You may experience some of the worst icing over mountains (most of it probably unforecast). Determine if the wind is moving the moisture up and over this terrain. Any mountain range can produce ice under the right conditions; it doesn't occur only over coastal mountain ranges.

The wave clouds created by cold frontal passage can be heavy ice makers.

## Pireps important

During the briefing, be sure to ask for pilot reports (pireps). When available, these can be the best source of current information. Typically, the pirep includes information on cloud tops and bases, and reported icing. Icing intensities are listed in pireps by the following definitions:
• Trace- ice becomes perceptible. The rate of accumulation is slightly greater than the rate of sublimation. The ice is not hazardous even though deicing/anti-icing equipment is not utilized, unless it is encountered for an extended period of time (over one hour).
• Light- the rate of accumulation may create a problem if the flight is prolonged in this environment for over one hour. Occasional use of deicing/anti-icing equipment removes and/or prevents accumulation. Ice does not present a problem if the deicing/anti-icing equipment is used.
• Moderate- the rate of ice accumulation is such that short encounters become potentially hazardous and the use of deicing/anti-icing equipment or diversion is necessary.
• Severe- the rate of ice accumulation is such that deicing/anti-icing equipment fails to reduce or control the hazard. Immediate diversion is necessary.

Pireps have drawbacks depending on the reporter. A major problem with these definitions is that what is trace icing for a B-727 may be severe icing for a Cessna 182 due to differences in speed and airframe/airfoil shapes. Another problem is that by the time you reach the area where the report was given, conditions could have altered drastically. Pireps can confirm forecast icing or indicate unforecast icing, but be cautious when using them.

Two other items that the briefer should mention are airmets and sigmets. An airmet is issued at the first indication of the presence of moderate icing and a sigmet is issued for severe icing.

## A practical example

We pulled together weather data for several days in late October. As you can see from the weather depiction chart on the next page, heavy frontal activity was generated by a low pressure system at the South Dakota and Nebraska borders. A warm front from the low stretched to the upper Great Lakes. Southward from the low, a cold front extended back into northern New Mexico and Arizona.

Compare the weather depiction chart with the radar summary chart

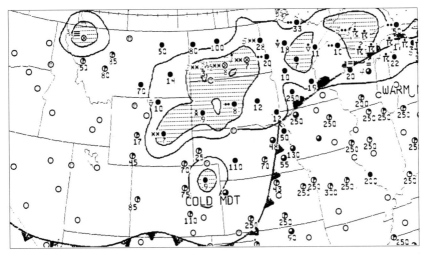

*The weather depiction chart (at 10Z) shows a low at the South Dakota and Nebraska borders, with a warm front stretching to the Upper Great Lakes and a cold front extending south and west back to Arizona.*

below to see the mixed bag of weather: thunderstorms, rain, snow, ice, low ceilings and visibilities, MVFR and IFR.

## Freezing level

Mentally overlay the icing and freezing level data from the area forecast on a map if you don't have access to the freezing level chart. On this day,

*The radar summary (1235Z) shows thunderstorms along the warm front into the Great Lakes. Show and rain showers trail the cold front.*

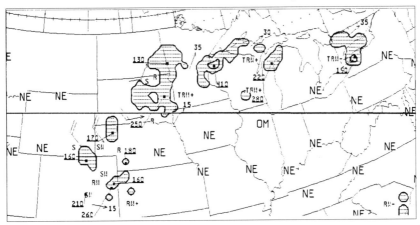

icing is forecast for the Dakotas, Nebraska, Minnesota, Iowa, Wisconsin, Michigan and Lakes Superior and Michigan. These areas are expecting occasional moderate mixed icing and precipitation in clouds above the freezing level to 16,000 feet. According to the area forecast, the freezing level varies from 6000 to 8000 feet north of a line from Rapid City, South Dakota, to Detroit, Michigan, and 10,000 to 13,000 feet south of that line. The outlook calls for the freezing level to lower to between 4000 and 6000 feet northwest of a line from Scottsbluff, Nebraska, to Marquette, Michigan, by 1800Z. By 2200Z, the freezing level will be at the surface over the Dakotas and western Nebraska.

You get a clearer picture by reviewing the freezing level panel below. The solid lines are contours of the lowest observed freezing level. These contours are in 4000-foot intervals and are labeled in hundreds of feet msl. Notice that the 8000-foot contour runs through the areas of heaviest frontal activity, so expect ice in the clouds at 8000 feet in those areas.

The next clue appears on the constant pressure (millibar) charts. The 850 millibar chart (next page) lists observations at approximately 5000 feet. Reporting stations are indicated on the charts by small circles, and a shaded circle represents a temperature/dew point spread of 5C or less, indicating moisture-laden air.

Temperatures are listed in the upper left corner of each observation. If it's between 0 and -10 C, ice is sure to be present, which is the case for several stations in the vicinity of the low.

## Lifting and stability

Lifting agents push the air rapidly upward, thereby causing the mois-

*Freezing level (12Z). The solid lines are contours of lowest freezing level. The 8000-foot contour runs through the heaviest frontal activity, so expect ice.*

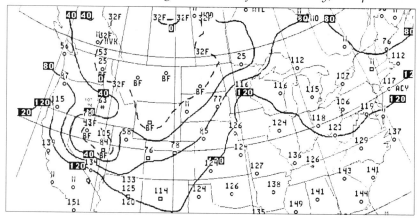

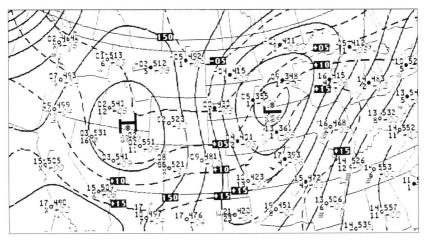

*The 850 millibar (5000 feet at 12Z) analysis shows darkened station circles around the low, indicating temperature/dew point stpreads of 5 C or less.*

ture in the air to condense into the supercooled drops that turn to ice on impact with an airframe. Lifting agents can include mountains, frontal and convective activity. In this case, there is considerable convective activity along the front, so icing can be expected.

The lifted/K index panel of the stability chart below indicates atmospheric moisture and stability. A positive lifted index (top value) indicates stable air, with high positive numbers meaning highly stable air. Negative index values ranging from 0 to -4 indicate areas of unstable

*The stability chart for 12Z shows a low lifted index and high K index over Wisconsin and negative lifted/high K indices ahead of the cold front.*

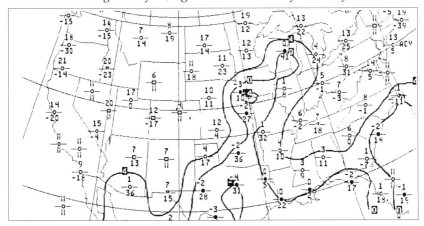

air (the potential for convection) with large negatives (-5 to -8) indicating very unstable air, meaning severe thunderstorms are likely.

The K index (bottom value) evaluates moisture and temperature, but should not be used as a true indicator of stability. Generally, the higher the K index, the greater the potential for moisture and an unstable lapse rate. A high K index indicates that air mass thunderstorms will develop during spring and summer. The K index is a less reliable indicator of thunderstorms in cooler months.

The lifted index chart shows low and negative lifted index values and high K index values ahead of both fronts. This means the conditions are favorable for thunderstorm development, possibly severe. Because of this high convective activity, ice formation is highly probable. Severe thunderstorms developed along the cold front as the low pressure system moved eastward.

## Forecast review

To determine what the system will do in the next few hours, carefully review the terminal, area, winds/temperatures aloft forecasts and also the low-level significant weather prognostic chart. If possible, obtain trend information. Review charts and reports from the previous reporting period(s) and note areas of moisture to determine if and when that moisture will move over your route.

Let's review the terminal forecasts for three airports around the front; Madison, Wisconsin—at the frontal boundary; Minneapolis-St. Paul—just behind the front; and Rapid City, South Dakota—some distance behind and west of the front.

Madison has an amended forecast at 0937Z, expecting ceilings between 1000 and 3000 feet, southerly winds, low visibilities in rain showers and thunderstorms. Minneapolis, also an amended forecast, is calling for the same, except for northwest winds. Rapid City is expecting low ceilings, snow and high northwest winds, with slow improvement to MVFR ceilings.

These three reports indicate that the front isn't moving rapidly, with little movement to the east expected for the next several hours. Any ice will probably stay in that area for a while.

## Prog charts

For a pictorial presentation, review the significant weather prognostic charts (next page), which illustrate the forecast weather for 12 and 24 hours.

There are extensive areas of forecast rain and snow showers (enclosed by smooth lines) just behind the warm front. This suggests large

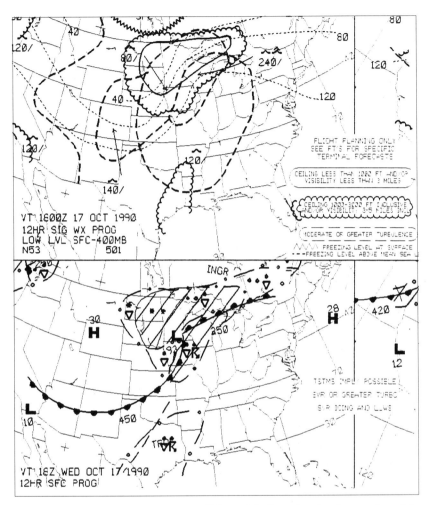

*12-hour significant weather prog valid at 18Z. Freezing levels are plotted in 4000-foot intervals on the top panel. On this chart, freezing levels are 4000 and 8000 feet near the fronts, making an icing encounter likely. Rain and snow showers are expected behind the warm front, inside the solid line. The dashed line indicates extensive moderate turbulence.*

areas of stratus clouds. Temperatures within these clouds change little, so descending or climbing within the cloud layer in order to find warmer, ice-free air may not work. But climbing above or descending a few thousand feet could get you out of the clouds entirely.

In the top panel, the forecast freezing levels are plotted in 4000-foot intervals for the highest level. On this chart, the forecast freezing levels remain low, and eventually descend to the surface, just along and behind the warm front.

When reviewing this chart, be especially alert for an upper freezing level contour that crosses the surface 32-degree line. This indicates multiple freezing levels due to layers of warmer air aloft, and when combined with clouds and precipitation, can also indicate the presence of ice.

Areas of forecast IFR/MVFR ceilings and turbulence are also indicated on the top panels. Note that they remain fairly constant throughout the period, with some movement to the east. Again, expect to encounter icing.

Ice is certainly going to be present in clouds and precipitation near the warm front, so flights through this area should proceed with caution.

## Essential elements

Remember the following when reviewing winter weather data for clues to the presence of ice:
• Expect ice in visible moisture and temperatures from 0 to -10 C.
• Thunderstorms can produce ice in warmer layers below the freezing level.
• Be alert for areas where the winds are moving over land from areas of open water, setting the stage for ice production in clouds. Large ice-producing regions are the Pacific Northwest, the Great Lakes and the East Coast when winds are easterly.
• Freezing levels can be multiple and slope with warm air in between levels. Always find out where the warmer air layers are just in case you need to make a quick escape. And when in ice-producing clouds, don't stay in them any longer than necessary. Climb or descend out of the clouds and/or into warmer air as necessary. The tops of stratus layer clouds tend to have more moisture, hence more ice.
• Give reports when you encounter ice. Usually, this is the only way forecasts can be verified.

Always remember that you're the taxpayer for the weather briefing system. Don't be bashful about asking the briefer for all information you need to make an informed decision.

*Icing is the big winter problem, the one that gets all the attention. However, snow can be just as dangerous in its own way. Unlike ice, many of the problems caused by snow occur not while in flight, but on the ground: everything from collisions with snowbanks (it happens more often than you might think) to loss of traction to snow-packed wheel pants.*

*Here's a close look at the white stuff, and what you can do about it.*

## Snow

The weather forecast at the destination was for marginal VFR conditions. The two pilots filed an IFR flight plan, since the flight would end in darkness. Once in flight, the conditions deteriorated each time they checked with Flight Watch.

As they neared their destination, the controller vectored them for the approach: "Centurion One-Two-Three-Lima-Fox, cleared for the localizer back course Runway 24 approach. Current weather, measured ceiling 1100 broken, visibility one mile in blowing snow. Wind 210 at 15. Braking action reported fair to poor by a pick-up truck."

The two pilots looked at each other and said, A pick-up truck? No other aircraft had landed recently to give a current report.

The air was smooth and when they turned on the wing lights, the reflection of millions of snowflakes shooting past the window was almost blinding. They flew the approach and spotted the runway in time. Buried in the snow, the runway lights shined through the white stuff, making it appear as an eerie glow.

There were no ground references to aid in depth perception, so the power was set with a fixed rate of descent on the VSI. They touched down as slowly as possible and applied left aileron for crosswind correction. The pick-up truck was right about the braking action. They would remember this flight for some time.

How could something so benign and gentle lead to a near disaster? Snow is one type of frozen precipitation, and while it's a child's plaything on the ground, to a pilot it can be as dangerous as ice.

Scientists and researchers classify snow into 10 different categories. For our purposes, we'll stick with the usual classifications of wet, which sticks to your airplane, and dry, which blows, drifts and causes poor visibility. Regardless of the category, each type of snow starts the same way.

## How it forms

Snow crystals develop only within a narrow set of atmospheric conditions. These conditions are clouds completely saturated with moisture, temperatures ranging from -12 to -20C and the presence of condensation nuclei, such as particles of salt, dirt, dust or smog. Any variation in these conditions produces ice, freezing rain or rain.

Supercooled water droplets in the clouds cling to these suspended particles, crystallize and grow. As the crystals move through the clouds via updrafts and downdrafts or fall to the ground, they can change form depending on the atmospheric conditions. For example, collisions with other snow crystals in the clouds create larger crystals, and snow falling through warmer air (such as in a front) can produce snow pellets, which are slightly melted snow crystals coated with ice.

This partially melted snow is particularly dangerous because of its relatively warm, wet and sticky nature. When hitting a cold airframe, wet snow takes on rime ice characteristics, since it is produced at about the same temperature as rime ice.

When wet snow impacts a cold airframe, it builds up tough-to-dislodge ridges along leading edges and ices up other areas of the fuselage. Anti-ice and de-ice protection can help, but this equipment may not be sufficient to get you through heavy wet snow for long periods of time. Aircraft anti-ice and de-ice equipment is tested to be effective against ice, not snow.

You'll find some snow in just about all parts of the country in the winter. Even the southern and southwestern states experience occasional snow storms and thunder-snow showers, and cloud cover over mountain ranges almost always contains snow in some form.

## Where to look

When flight planning, be alert to any mention of snow in addition to ice in surface observations, as well as terminal and area forecasts. Check the surface analysis, weather depiction, temperatures and winds aloft, significant weather and moisture stability charts for current conditions and find out where the moisture might be headed. Pay particular attention to the location of fronts and the temperatures associated with them, as these are ripe breeding grounds for wet snow. In general, any area where there may be ice (temperatures between 0 and -20C), there can also be snow.

The National Weather Service classifies snow as light, moderate or heavy. These classifications are determined by visibility rather than rate of accumulation. Light snow is any reported amount, moderate snow restricts visibility to less than 5/8 of a mile but not less than 5/16 of a mile and heavy snow restricts visibility to less than 5/16 of a mile.

Check the remarks section of weather reports when snow is observed. You'll find the rate of accumulation, how much has accumulated and how much is already on the ground. If you have access to printed reports, you will see a term such as SNOINCR 2/7/10, which means the snow is increasing at a rate of two inches per hour, seven inches have accumulated in the last six hours and there is a total of 10 inches on the ground.

Total snow depths on the ground are included as five-digit codes in reports issued at 0300Z, 0900Z, 1500Z, and 2100Z. This code, which always starts with 904, is issued in addition to the above report so that you can see the exact amount on the ground even if it's stopped snowing. An example: the code 90410 indicates a total of 10 inches of snow on the ground. In mountainous areas, it's not unusual to find more than 100 inches on the ground, but hopefully not on the runway. This is indicated by two codes, such as 90499 90410, meaning 110 inches on total snow ground cover. In the first code, 99 indicates 100 inches, then add the second code 10, to receive 110 inches. Snow cover in excess of 200 inches will be indicated by three 904 reports. Again, add the values to receive the total.

Snow notams are issued for some larger airports when snow conditions affect operations. In particular, you'll want to be alert to runway conditions and plowing activities. Notams may not be issued for your destination airport if it doesn't have a control tower or flight service station. In this case, it's a good idea to call before departing and get an update on runway conditions.

You may fly your entire life and never be affected by snow in flight. Chances are greater that you'll certainly have to deal with it on the ground. Whether in the air or on the ground, operating in snow takes a bit more caution and preplanning on your part. Use common sense and don't put yourself into a situation where there's no escape.

# Index